I0363909

# ... a figment of your imagination, my dear

a memoir

## Elizabeth Mamchak

A figment of your imagination, my dear
Paperback ISBN 978 1 76109 716 4
ebook ISBN 978 1 76109 717 1
Copyright © Elizabeth Mamchak 2026
Typesetting by Rack and Rune Publishing
Cover artwork by Barnaby McBryde

First published 2026 by
**GINNINDERRA PRESS**
PO Box 2 Bentleigh 3204
ginninderrapress.com.au

*For my son, Andrew*
*Your help has been fundamental in shaping my story*
*and bringing it to light*

*For all survivors of incest and child sexual abuse*

Not everything that is faced
   can be changed;
but nothing can be changed
until it is faced.

      James Baldwin

# Introduction

*At the time my father abused me, incest was publicly dismissed and hugely underestimated, even though there are records dating back to the time of colonisation. Certainly, sexual abuse was neither discussed nor recognised as the pervasive problem it is now known to be. Society's norms were patriarchal, and sexism was the norm. This remained so until the women's movement raised awareness of child sexual abuse in the 1970s.*

*The women's movement pushed for the recognition of child abuse and incest, overcoming the backlash of the False Memory Syndrome and challenging the climate of denial. As a child of the 1940s and 1950s, I was of an era where denial was the norm. It took decades to understand that incest is not only a crime but also the root cause of the mental health problems I have struggled with for much of my life.*

*When I ask myself, which I do reasonably often, why I persist in telling my story, my answer lies in the deeply held conviction that all abuse thrives within a climate of silence. In addition, my experience has been that fear maintains this silence, especially when the abuse starts at an early age and the child is dependent and malleable. Research supports this view.*

*If I don't leave an account of the reasons for the grief and anguish I have suffered, then it will have been for nothing. I might as well say 'go on you sexual predators who use children for your depraved impulses and inflict your special form of damage so that your victims live a lifetime of fear, self-doubt, depression and a distorted view of themselves.'*

*I can only describe what I remember. I have significant gaps in memory for events that took place through much of my life. Where there are incomplete memory fragments, that is what I shall describe, as memory fragments are very much part of the trauma narrative.*

*I have been surprised at how much I have learnt while writing my story. The pattern of my behaviour in the first decades of my adult life surely reveals that something was very amiss. The knowledge wasn't yet available for the many child sexual abuse survivors like me to make sense of the craziness that inhabited our worlds. Looking at the different chapters of my life, whether determined by location or by marriage, what has stood out is that the course of my life had an inevitability about it that I could not have foreseen at the time. The depression, the never-ending fear and peaks of panic, the flashbacks and nightmares, and the severe postnatal depression all signalled that something was very wrong but didn't hint at a solution. I tried to keep putting one foot in front of the other. It has taken me a lifetime to draw all the threads together and to form a more complete picture.*

*This is my personal story. I hope it also contributes to the current discussion of child sexual abuse. It highlights some of the difficulties for survivors born in the 1940s and 1950s. Recent events have again shone a spotlight on sexual violence against women and children, and women are demonstrating a determination to be heard. They are demanding change across the board. The remarkable and inspiring Grace Tame, 2021 Australian of the Year, is a sexual assault survivor, activist and advocate for survivors of sexual abuse. Grace is a strong voice for survivors. I am sure I was not alone in shedding tears of joy as I watched her win being announced on television. Grace gave a very powerful address at the Press Club and has stated on numerous occasions that to solve the problem of sexual abuse there must be a conversation, and that conversation must be informed by the stories of sexual abuse survivors. She also warns against sanitising the stories of abuse as this only serves to protect perpetrators. The women's movement continues to gain momentum on the back of women's anger.*

*Lack of knowledge halted my own recovery and caused me to blame myself for all the destructive events that occurred in my life, events that were in fact connected to the damage caused by the abuse. My father held positions of power in the government, and that power was a very real impediment to disclosing my abuse and believing I would be heard. He exercised this power in the home with controlling, patriarchal and authoritarian behaviour. And incest.*

*If my story raises any issues for the reader, please seek help from a trusted person. A first point of contact could be one of the helplines, a general practitioner or a women's service listed at the end of the book. There is so much knowledge available today about how trauma can affect the individual and a greater understanding of how to assist those suffering from the effects of sexual violence. Many credible, well researched books are readily available to help make sense of the damage inflicted and to place the blame where it rightly belongs – on the perpetrator.*

# Prologue

'So... how many Greeks are you fucking at the moment?' my father asked after we were seated at a table in the Canberra airport bar. It was the early seventies, and I had driven him to the airport to catch his business flight. We were waiting for the flight to be called. I didn't answer, feeling a blanket of shame and confusion settle over me. This sort of question always elicited an entirely emotional response. I never knew quite what to do with it. I can only imagine now, over fifty years later, that he would have derived as much gratification from my obvious discomfort as from a response. Perhaps more.

It didn't occur to me that this question was completely unacceptable and indeed misogynistic, offensive and belittling both to me and my Greek employers. I was in my late twenties, mother of two young children, separated from my husband, and proud that I had gained a full-time job as a waitress at a pizzeria in Manuka, an upmarket shopping centre in Canberra, after an emotionally harrowing time. It was my first step to financial independence. My hope was that it would allow me to pay the mortgage on my house, and have my children back with me once again. Tragically, I never did get my children back. All our lives, including that of my third and youngest child, not then born, were deeply affected. But then, I was just trying to survive any way I could. I was proud that I had overcome a shaky first few days on the job and could now serve a full contingent of customers at lunchtime when it was particularly busy and make coffees for the afternoon tea crowd.

It would be another twenty odd years, when I was in my late forties, before I asserted myself decisively with my father in response to one of his many derisive comments. By then I was working in my chosen profession of social work, sober (although still on medication), married (unsuccessfully) for a third time and mothering my youngest child – in her early teens – in the best way I knew how. I also had contact with my two older children.

It was the late eighties and my husband, my daughter and I were having dinner at my father's house in Red Hill so that I could catch up with my sister who was visiting Canberra and staying with my father. As usual, we sat around the dining table after our meal, talking. The subject of HIV/AIDS arose in the course of conversation. I cannot remember what triggered it, but ultimately there was a very heated exchange between my sister and my father, with opposing views on the likelihood of AIDS becoming an epidemic. My father regarded this as fanciful. My sister became visibly upset. She was, after all, a doctor who lived in America and had witnessed an increase in the spread of the virus and the accompanying global fear, resulting from a lack of knowledge about the origins of the condition, and consequently a lack of appropriate treatment. My sister became distressed by my father's inability to accept the medical viewpoint she was putting forward, and she left to go for a walk. At this point my father turned to me and asked, mockingly, 'Why are you two so neurotic?' I replied, without thinking, 'Because of my parents.' I took a deep breath and added 'and don't you call me "a little bitch" ever again.' This was his preferred putdown when trying to undermine me; a wound that had been festering within for decades.

There was a long silence. Then, my father said in a very cold and steely voice, as he traced the perimeters of his placemat methodically with the tips of his fingers, 'you will take your husband, and your daughter, and you will leave my house. And I will not be coming to your place for dinner tomorrow evening.' I had invited my family of origin for a meal while my sister was in Canberra. I replied, with some bravado, 'First I will find my sister and say goodbye to her.' However, I could not find her, and so my husband, my daughter and I all drove home. I cried all the way.

To this day I don't understand what or who the tears were for.

PART ONE

**Growing up**

# Beginnings

I was born in Canberra in 1944, on 9 January, my father's birthday. Perhaps this gave him a greater sense of ownership over me. It caused me distress.

I was the middle child, my sister being almost three years older and my brother almost four years younger. My mother told me that I was born in a private hospital that later became the Sri Lankan High Commission. My birth certificate says I was born in The Canberra Community Hospital, located on the Acton peninsula, now the site of the Australian Museum. This small discrepancy is of no significance. It is but one of the many details, amongst other matters, that I wish I'd raised with my mother when I returned to Canberra to live in the early seventies. I wasn't ready to broach deeply personal issues with her then and I question how receptive she might have been anyway. We tacitly agreed to avoid touchy subjects. In 1974, while my mother was visiting my sister and her family in Palo Alto, California, my sister, a doctor, detected an abnormality in my mother's breast, and on her return to Australia my mother was diagnosed with breast cancer. She died less than a year later, at the age of sixty-one. Our relationship wasn't close, and I believe I was a great disappointment to her. I think subconsciously she hoped to achieve some of her lost dreams through me.

When I think of my past, I tend to carve it into chunks of time according to where I was living. I lived in the family home in Durville Crescent, Griffith in Canberra, from when I was born until shortly before I turned nine. I attended kindergarten, followed by the first four years of schooling, at the Church of England Girls Grammar School in Deakin. It puzzles me that I remember so little of these early years. Certainly, there are those 'told' memories of events that are repeated so often at family gatherings that it's easy to imagine being part of them. My years in Canberra are, on the whole, hazy. When my father was dying and in a coma, I remember my sister Pam saying to an old family friend who had come to say goodbye to him that she had fond memories of her early years in Canberra. This remark lodged in my brain, and I have since wondered just what constituted these 'fond memories'. What made them so warm and loving? And who featured in these memories?

I have some visual pictures of random events that happened in those early years, but there is an absence of feeling associated with them. I'm puzzled by this lack of feeling. I can't remember a single Christmas, and birthdays exist only in shared family memories. What is even more disturbing is that I am unable to place my mother at the centre of any significant happenings, even though she didn't work and would have been present for my day-by-day activities. I have no memory of being in the kitchen while she cooked or sitting at the dining table for a family meal but she would often sing to me at bedtime...

> *It's a long way to Tipperary... it's a long way to go. It's a long way to Tipperary, to the sweetest girl I know! Goodbye Piccadilly. Farewell Leicester Square! It's a long long way to Tipperary, but my heart's right there.*

A friend who lived next door told me that Peg, my mother, took us to see the fires on Red Hill in 1952. I have no conscious memory of this terrifying event, but my body held a memory that surfaced again during the 2003 Canberra fires. I recall the relief I felt when my father was at 't'office' or away on an overseas trip. And I remember the fear I felt around him, such that his absence was always a reprieve.

My mother would often tell the story of how one afternoon I arrived home from school in my Grammar uniform minus a shoe but with a bunch of flowers for her. She loved this story; a somewhat bedraggled child, holding out a bunch of dandelions, as she stepped onto the front porch of the house in Durville Crescent. It was clear I wanted to please my mother. Another telling occasion was that of the birthday present I chose for my mother one September. I was probably about six. I selected screw-on earrings in the shape of a flower, with a clear diamond coloured centre and turquoise petals. I bought them at Woolworths in Kingston and thought they were the most beautiful earrings in the whole wide world. My excitement was completely shattered when my father declared them to be 'cheap and nasty'. Decades later, my eldest daughter pointed out their true value when I told her I found one of the earrings, nestled amongst my mother's jewellery, when I was sorting through her personal possessions and clothing after her death.

I have a small collection of little black-and-white photos, typical of the 1950s and 1960s, as a limited record of my years in Canberra. As I examine them, I notice how often my sister and I were dressed as twins. We were much the same height despite the age difference. I know immediately the colours of the clothes we were wearing but this knowledge fails to complete the picture.

Where were we? What were we doing? Who was taking the photo and why? Were we happy or sad, excited or bored? It is the detail intrinsic to the photo that I crave, to give it depth and meaning. In one photo, with Wollongong written on the back, I see I am holding hands with my sister. This is quite a revelation for me. We were not at all demonstrative as a family and this gesture of holding hands raises some more questions. Was I close to my sister? Was she protective of me?

In these early years I have a clear memory of feeling shame. I would have been about three and a half and I remember pushing open my parents' bedroom door to see my mother standing naked, and hugely pregnant, in front of her dressing table mirror. I don't remember anything being said, but somehow, she communicated to me that I had done something I shouldn't have done and had seen something I shouldn't have seen. I backed out of the room feeling terribly ashamed. Shame has followed me persistently through much of my life.

At the end of 1952 we left Canberra, as a family, for Switzerland, where my father was to take up the position of Treasurer of the International Labour Organisation. We travelled by ship to Genoa and then to Geneva by train. I am astonished that I don't have endless memories of this move. It would have been a transformative adventure for an almost nine-year-old girl. The one strange little memory I do have is of feeling acutely disappointed that the train platform on the Swiss side of the border wasn't immaculately clean, as everyone in Australia had promised. Everyone said 'Switzerland is just so clean'. I felt very let down that this wasn't so.

*On the front porch of our house at Durville Crescent,
Pam on the left, me on the right*

*Pam (right) and me (left) dressed as twins, Wollongong, January 1952*

# The Move to Geneva

On our arrival in Geneva we stayed in a hotel until we found a house to rent. My vague memory of the hotel is that it was old-fashioned and stylish. I would probably have described it as posh. We soon moved into a house located in the outskirts of Geneva. The house was called La Pallanterie and it had a gravel driveway with rose bushes either side leading from the long road which ran in front of the house up to the village. La Pallanterie had two storeys with a distinctive porthole-shaped window on the right-hand side, which marked my parents' ensuite. The driveway continued through an archway onto a paved square. On the sides of the square were the main house, the maid's quarters, with red and white gingham curtains, and a long concrete horse trough for plants. The fourth side of the square was open land with a large tree under which I remember playing 'shops'. It was all very rustic. There was a cherry orchard reaching out from the back. My father once chased my sister Pam through the orchard in a rare outburst of anger.

Across the road there was a field, at the edge of which was a wooded area. Hidden amongst the trees was an old stone ruin of what we children believed had been a castle, as there was a moat around it. It was a wonderfully frightening place to play in as it had a spooky feel to it. Our imagination took flight and we conjured up all sorts of bloodthirsty incidents as we made our way through the silent and ominously gloomy undergrowth.

From the living room of the house we could see the distinct shape of the snow-covered Mont Blanc, the highest mountain in the

Alps and Western Europe, rising majestically in the distance across the border into France. My parents had an expansive bedroom with long floor-to-ceiling sliding doors that opened onto a private balcony. My older sister had the largest remaining bedroom. My brother has always claimed he was given the boxroom. I had the fourth, small and decidedly unremarkable bedroom.

I have a number of memories from the time we lived in this house. The first is when I opened the door to the dining room during a party my parents were holding, soon after moving in, to see my father passionately kissing a female colleague from the International Labour Organisation. I backed out without being heard, feeling shocked and betrayed. The second memory is of my mother washing my long hair in the bath, and telling me all about menstrual periods, before I was to leave for three weeks to learn French at a pensionnat in the mountains. I couldn't see her face and the exchange of information was decidedly uncomfortable. I was nine years old. A more humorous memory is how my brother, at the tender age of six, decided he wanted to wear glasses for some reason. He used the view of Mont Blanc from the living room window to highlight his failing vision, declaring that he couldn't quite make out the sharp outlines of this very distinctive mountain. It was really very blurry. My mother was initially concerned about Philip's eyesight but soon saw through this ruse and caught him out midst great hilarity. We lived in this house for a year before moving into a large, four-storeyed house at 89 Route de Chêne, in Geneva, just up the road from Ecolint, the International School I attended with my siblings.

When I started school at Ecolint, I was told by my class teacher, 'don't worry, you will probably catch up with your sister in no time.' I was bemused by this comment, as my sister was almost three years older than me, and I had no wish or expectation to be in the same class as her. I can only explain this comment by the fact that my sister and I were much the same size and had been mistaken for twins. And yet, surely the school would have noted that we were born two years and ten months apart?

I reached puberty at the age of ten, something that finally made sense when I read Bessel van der Kolk's book, *The Body Keeps the Score*. Van der Kolk states that 'The abused, isolated girls with incest histories mature sexually a year and a half earlier than the non-abused girls. Sexual abuse speeds up their biological clocks and the secretion of sex hormones. Early in puberty the abused girls had three to five times the levels of testosterone and androstenedione, the hormones that fuel sexual desire, as the girls in the control group.' My early development, noticeably advanced compared to my classmates, is evident in the old school photos from this time. Further research was published in *The Journal of Adolescent Health* in 2017, which supports the findings that girls sexually abused in childhood achieve puberty earlier than their non-abused peers.

Memories of the years living in the house on Route de Chêne are mixed. The abuse, which had started many years before, continued silently, and so I lived in this strange world with two realities which had to be kept separate in order to function. School was in every way an enriching experience. With students from more than sixty countries, it was a space free of prejudice and bigotry and judgement. It was indeed an international community. Depending on which exams you were taking, students learnt in either English or French. As I was taking the English General Certificate of Education exams for university entrance, I was on the English side. I made friends easily and never lacked companionship. I performed more than adequately in class and my results were above average. But as I moved into my teenage years, I became confused about who I was and what I wanted to achieve in my life. From an early age, my sister knew she wanted to study medicine. I had no such clear ambition and dithered around, always choosing some aspect of female appearance to focus on, like hairdressing or dress design, when in reality, I had little genuine interest in these professions. My father must have decided I was bright enough to go to university and I was steered firmly in this direction even though I had no clear idea of a future career at that stage.

In June 1953, when I was ten, my class was herded from our middle school building over to the assembly hall in the main building, to watch Queen Elizabeth's coronation on a black-and-white television. It was there that I experienced my first panic attack. As I sat on the floor with my classmates in the crowded hall, I couldn't breathe, became shaky and lightheaded, and felt as though I would pass out. I was taken outside to sit on the steps of the entrance to the hall and told to put my head between my legs.

Around that time, I recall going into my classroom in the middle school and being overwhelmed by such a raucous cacophony of noise that, in a flash of bright red anger, I picked up a schoolbag and slammed it over the head of one of the boys. There ensued a physical fight, with John, my unwitting target, grabbing my ponytail, whirling me around and hitting me across the nose so blood spurted forth. Teachers were called and John was reprimanded, while I was shown nothing but sympathy. My mother was called to the school, and she took me home to recover. It was terribly unfair as I had instigated the fight with no provocation. Normally extremely compliant, I had occasions of unfathomable rage.

In that large house on Route de Chêne when I was ten years old, my father would creep into my room at night and molest me by penetrating me vaginally with his fingers. I would pretend to be asleep, but I kept my bedroom door open an exact amount every night, so that I could hear the distinctive click of the door when he crept in and shut it. That same distinctive click was replicated in the house I lived in with my daughter and third husband in Fisher, Canberra, some forty years later, triggering memories of the early abuse. At this same age, I became obsessive about not stepping on the cracks in the pavement when I walked to school and carefully tidying and adjusting everything not put away in a cupboard in my bedroom, every night before turning out the light. I might rearrange my shoes four or five times before I was satisfied that they were perfectly aligned. The same compulsion hovered around the precise amount my bedroom door was left open, to let in the hall light and warn me of my father's arrival.

As I revisit in my mind these houses in which I grew up, I am surprised by how little evidence there is of me in my bedrooms. In the big house in Route de Chêne, my bedroom was beautifully furnished with elegant antique furniture, a chaise longue covered in pink satin and a matching pink bedspread. Nothing revealed who I was as a person. The only sign that I inhabited this personal space was a collection of dainty glass horses and various china and glass animals which were locked behind the glass doors of a wall cabinet.

In this same house in Geneva, my father would demand that I sit on his knee. 'C'mon Ish,' he would say, patting his knee. Then, while chatting to whosoever might also be in the living room we called the green salon, he would move me around, or back and forth, on his knee and I could feel his erection on my buttocks and thighs. I was way too big to be sitting on his knee and we had never had this sort of relationship anyway. A perfunctory goodnight kiss on the cheek was the full extent of our public display of affection. However, such was my fear of him, I could neither refuse to sit on his knee nor make excuses to get off.

One of the ways I made friends in those first years at Ecolint was around a shared love of animals. Two American friends and I joined forces to establish a dog club in whose name we held a fete to raise money for the equivalent of the RSPCA. We would regularly take our dogs for long walks along a beautiful little stream near one of my friends' homes. For my twelfth birthday, friends arranged a surprise birthday present of two little budgerigars which were kept hidden in their cage in a room on the top level of our house. I couldn't contain myself and sneaked quietly upstairs to find out what the mystery present was. I was bitterly disappointed as, at that stage of my life, I didn't like birds at all. When the day of my birthday came, I was in tears and wanted to cancel it. I didn't want a birthday with a surprise gift that I already knew about and having to pretend I loved it. I was in the green salon, near the fireplace, crying and protesting that I didn't want a birthday party. My father ignored my tears and protests, grabbed my hand on the mantlepiece, and twisted it back on itself so that it really hurt, and said to me, with quiet menace, 'You will greet your friends, and you will be a gracious hostess to them.'

This is also the house where the infamous story of the silver whistle, which was reported in one of the many eulogies for my father, occurred. My father decided that because the house was so large, with its four levels and a basement, he would use a whistle to summon us rather than shouting our names. My mother was included in this new regime and each of us was allocated a number of blasts on the whistle. This practice was introduced with great mirth and must have been talked about by all and sundry, as my father was given a silver whistle when he left the International Labour Organisation. I never found it funny. To me, like much of my father's humour, I found it demeaning, although I could not have articulated this thought at the time.

My mother is, once again, an obscure figure during the eight years in Geneva, even though she would have been present in my daily life. What I know of her is derived largely through the recollections of my siblings, my brother in particular. We would return to Australia for home leave every two years. Apart from one trip by plane, we always travelled by ship as, I understand, my mother was afraid of flying. I can understand that fear but I think that above all, my mother loved the relaxed and friendly life aboard the Lloyd Triestino ships we travelled on. For her it was a complete holiday, during which we children were always happily occupied with table tennis or swimming in the little pool. There was a sparkle and energy about her on these trips and I have wondered if there were other factors contributing to her state of being. My father didn't come on the home leave ship voyages, as they took over a month to reach Australia and the same for the return trip. I didn't join the last home leave trip in early 1959 as my sister was returning to start her university course in medicine and I had to prepare for my O-levels. I stayed in Geneva with my father.

*Our house just up the road from Ecolint,*
*89 Route de Chêne, Geneva*

# Life at Ecolint

Ecolint was unique, its distinctive features reflecting the environment in which it was located, namely that of the United Nations and other associated international organisations. We learnt about the United Nations by participating in the annual Students United Nations (SUN) and we devoted one day a year – Refugee Day – to raising money for refugees. The money raised was presented to a delegate from The High Commission for Refugees. The spirit of Ecolint was absorbed through activities such as these. Students were also active in putting together and publishing the yearbook, being involved in organising the dances for the senior students and participating in sports and drama. My only claim to fame was being made a monitor (as we called our prefects) in my senior years.

One of our duties as monitors was to call out students who smoked, but as I was a smoker by then, I managed to sidestep this responsibility. As seniors we would congregate at 'Grange', the name we students gave the local coffee shop where we drank coffee, smoked cigarettes and gossiped. It was exciting being part of the in-crowd. I had plenty of friends and was always going steady with one boy or another. Going steady was very American. In our younger years we would swap ID bracelets and make out, and the boy would carry the girl's books as he accompanied her on the walk home. My first official boyfriend was Ross Ardrey, who cheerfully took on the role of escorting me home. My mother recalled with some amusement how we would sit in silence in the sunroom at our house at Route de Chêne. I have no idea what we talked about, or if we did indeed talk. And yet somehow, I knew Ross was the son of well-known American playwright and author Robert Ardrey.

Many of my fellow students had some fascinating connection to fame and celebrity – even minor European royalty. Kerry Kelly was the daughter of Gene Kelly, actor and dancer, remembered even now for his lead role in the movie *Singin' in the Rain*. Kerry was the dead spit of her father. She was in my class for two years until she sat American university entrance exams while I pursued the English equivalent. With her twinkly eyes, wavy dark brown hair and enviably compact figure, I felt jealous of Kerry with her endless combinations of matching belts and flatties in every colour of the rainbow. She would wear these with a variety of different skirts. An Australian friend, with whom I shared my envy, and who also boarded at the school with a room near Kerry's, took me furtively up to the boarding section of the school and quietly opened the door to Kerry's wardrobe revealing pair upon pair of flatties. They were neatly positioned and lined up on the floor in every colour imaginable. Absorbing this display of excess was enough to quieten my jealousy.

The family backgrounds of students ranged from well-off to extremely affluent. Some students were rich in ways I had never encountered. Abdullah, for example, was a nephew of the then King Ibn Saud of Saudi Arabia and had been brought up in unbelievable wealth. Abdullah was in my class, and he had a rebellious side that challenged all the teachers. He was with a group of classmates one summer as we congregated at the plage – our beach on the edge of

Lac Leman. The plage consisted of a vast expanse of lawn. Although the lake water was cold and unappealing, it was a good place to socialise during the long summer months. Abdullah borrowed my watch and managed to lose it. I was upset. I couldn't afford to replace the watch until I saved enough money, and I relied on it. I consoled myself with the knowledge that Abdullah, with his vast wealth, would surely replace it, perhaps with something markedly superior to my basic but adequate model. I waited in anticipation but no... no replacement watch. Not even an apology.

Eventually Abdullah was expelled from the school as he proved too difficult to handle. This was after the headmaster had, we learnt, been presented with a magnificent jewelled dagger, by officials from Saudi Arabia in a ceremony to thank the school for educating Abdullah. Among my memories of Abdullah were of him crawling on his stomach, commando style, under the bushes around the main quadrangle, in full camouflage gear. And of him sitting in a tree smoking and flicking the ash on passers-by, not even trying to hide.

We held dances at Ecolint – Bal de Fin to celebrate the end of year and Bal de l'Escalade, the December festival that commemorated the failed assault by the Catholic Duke of Savoy on Protestant Geneva in 1602. Students enjoyed the preparations and putting up the decorations for these important occasions. Predictably, the girls were preoccupied with what they would wear. The dances were noisy and colourful, the music was of the era and the excitement intense. We also had quieter afternoon gatherings in private homes where we would dance to popular music starting with vigorous rock'n'roll and ending with slow ballads. We danced to singers like Elvis Presley, Frankie Laine, The Everly Brothers and Fats Domino. These afternoon get-togethers were held in our middle school years and were all about dancing cheek-to-cheek and exploring our burgeoning hormones in a safe way.

Uniforms were not worn at Ecolint, and fashion generally followed the American trends as depicted in *Seventeen* and other glossy magazines. Full skirts in a wide-ranging palette of colours, accentuated with layers of crinolines and cinched at the waist by belts, with matching flatties, were all the rage. The girls' fashion had a slightly competitive feel but I sewed some of my skirts and never felt out of place. Appearance was all-important to me. I never felt valued for my intelligence. I didn't think anyone cared about my opinions. I had long ago handed that baton to my sister.

Somewhere along the line, I must have been praised for how I looked, so I channelled all my energy into my appearance. I knew I was attractive to boys and, from my early teens, to men. It was something I accepted. It was the only asset I had any confidence in and it dominated my life. It was through my attraction to boys, and later men, that I sought reassurance of my worth.

I regularly had a love interest through my years at Ecolint, and this made me feel popular. One of my boyfriends was named Carlos Phillips. Carlos was in the same class as me and we went steady for a short time when I was fourteen. In recent years, I learned that he was the director of the Dolores Olmedo Museum, which houses the largest collection of Frida Kahlo and Diego Rivera's art. The museum began when Dolores Olmedo purchased the site for the museum in 1962 and converted it into a museum in 1994. Dolores Olmedo was a Mexican philanthropist, art collector and friend of Frida Kahlo and Diego Rivero. Diego painted her several times. Dolores is described by Claudia Herrera Hudson in her contribution to the blog, 'My Hero', as a much-admired Mexican woman who was independent and who forged her own path in life. I also discovered, to my great surprise, that Dolores was Carlos Philips' mother.

My fascination with Frido Kahlo and her husband Diego Rivera was ignited when I saw the movie *Frida* with my daughter Kate in Auckland soon after its release in 2002. I was more captivated by Kahlo's powerful and courageous story, and her volatile relationship with Rivera, than I was by their art. The past connection to Carlos gave the story another layer of meaning.

The one exception to an otherwise benign exploration of relationships, was an American boy who was at least a couple of classes ahead of me and only at Ecolint for a short time, with whom I fell madly 'in lust'. Reese was built like an American footballer and the epitome of 'cute' American style. He was enormously charismatic and he knew it, taking full advantage of his sexiness. I think he was stringing along a number of girls at the same time. Among this harem were a couple of Swedish girls, who were older, attractive in the blonde Scandinavian manner, and who had the reputation of being 'fast and loose'. I found them fascinating. Somehow, Reese was also attracted to me, and managed to engage me in a dalliance that was purely physical and always secretive. I even went to his church on Sundays so I could sit next to him and hold hands. I have a vivid memory of making out passionately with him in one of those clunky, old-fashioned cage-like elevators. Where we were going, I have no idea, but Reese knew how to manage a purely physical liaison with great aplomb. I would literally go weak at the knees when I was with him.

Despite never feeling valued for my intelligence, I was still expected to do well at school, a contradiction of sorts. I achieved good results, as my school reports – which my father kept – show, yet I never had the encouragement and stimulation of intellectual curiosity as a means of learning and acquiring knowledge. I missed out on a whole dimension of being inspired to learn.

I have difficulty retaining facts. My mind is hijacked by fear when I try to remember cold, hard facts. I can hear my father saying, as he thumped the dining table, 'Just give me the facts,' at which point my mind would go blank and my stomach would tighten like a vice.

Like most people, I compensated for what I felt I could not do by focusing on what I could. I was drawn to the human sciences as I had a fascination with understanding why people behave as they do, which led to a major in psychology and psychiatric social work at university. But in my GCEs I failed history. My inability to remember facts was highlighted by my answer to an exam question about the degree to which animals thrived and gained weight during the agricultural revolution. I couldn't remember by exactly how much their weight had increased, so, after a short deliberation, I massively exaggerated the number, thinking this would impress the examiners. I failed the paper roundly. I did, however, achieve good passes in six O-level subjects including Latin, which was enough for university entrance. I then achieved two A-level subjects in French and German, by completing the usual two years in one year, thus cementing my place at Sydney

University and a Commonwealth Scholarship. This was a good achievement for someone whose mind was usually on what to wear or which boy she was keen on.

When I look at the yearbooks for my senior years and read the messages written in them, I notice how light and funny and warm and affectionate they all are. We talk about how much fun we have had and how much we will miss each other. We were on the cusp of plunging into a new chapter of our lives and our excitement about the future alternated with sadness at saying goodbye.

Ecolint offered a unique environment in which students viewed life from a global perspective way before globalisation became the trend. Many of the students I knew contributed internationally or excelled in the arts. I am aware that we came from well-off backgrounds, but we were nonetheless able to take universal ideals of peace and respect for individual rights, and in particular, respect for diversity and gender, back to our country of origin and continue to practise them within our individual communities.

Despite these aspirational values, the hard truths of our young lives often told a different story. This was the case for me, projecting confidence as I walked through school with a smile on my face, ignoring the dark reality that lived at home.

*With Carlos Phillips Olmedo, my boyfriend at the time*

*Pam (centre-left) and me (centre-right)
in the garden outside Route de Chêne before the Bal de Fin,
Ecolint 1958*

# Memories of Europe

Growing up in Europe had many privileges and advantages. I learnt to speak French and German, and developed a love of language which persists to this day. I find the sounds and rhythm of the different languages enormously appealing even if I don't understand them.

Winter sports were part of living in Switzerland and while not naturally a sporty person, I enjoyed and did reasonably well at skating. The elegance of movement gliding across the ice appealed, like the grace I loved in dance. We had family holidays in the mountains in Austria and Germany during the Christmas break, usually shared with another Australian family who had been posted to Europe by the Australian government. The three daughters were of similar ages to my siblings and me. We shared many holidays with this family, including a memorable stay in Italy and Venice. Among the family photos is a series of striking black-and-white pictures of my brother and the youngest daughter of our companion family in silhouette on a rainy day feeding the pigeons in St Mark's Square.

My mother loved Italy, so we had some wonderful holidays in coastal villages on the Mediterranean and the Adriatic seas where we spent lazy hours on the beach soaking up the sun. Towards the end of the day, we would join the throng of families on the promenade as they strolled along the seafront. In Cattolica, on the Adriatic coast, I listened entranced to the locals singing old Italian folk songs in the evening. I loved the music, the unselfconscious talent of the songsters and the haunting melodies telling of love and loss.

Another cherished memory of Switzerland is visiting the mountains in the spring and picking bunches and bunches of wild narcissus with my mother and a good friend of hers. It was a magical setting and being allowed to pick as many of these sweetly scented blooms as we wanted to was extraordinary to me. I would have been eleven or twelve at the time and I was overwhelmed by the fields of wildflowers stretching out over the undulating hills. It was a moment straight out of *The Sound of Music*, before the movie existed!

In the northern summer of our first year in Geneva I was sent to a pensionnat in the mountains as a 'sink or swim' intensive in learning French. I was only nine, although I looked at least twelve or thirteen. There were advantages to looking older but also distinct disadvantages. I was seen as being older and expected to be correspondingly capable. At the pensionnat we would go swimming in the afternoons in a freezing cold swimming pool. Our reward was a hunk of bread and a generous portion of chocolate which we ate together. The combination was delicious. I learnt enough French to get by and continued to improve over the years.

The program at the pensionnat included an overnight hike. This hike turned out to be a mountaineering expedition, climbing Dents du Midi (the Teeth of Midday). We stayed overnight in a cabin where we slept on the wooden floor of a large, barnlike room. On our arrival, after a long and exhausting trek from the pensionnat, we were given a mug of what I thought was hot chocolate. Being tired and cold, I took in a large mouthful and swallowed. It was milk coffee! I loathed milk and had not yet acquired a taste for coffee, and I had to fight a strong impulse to vomit. The cabin was spartan and there was no toilet. We went outside to pee in the nearby paddock. Because we had to climb over each other to get outside, I became very nervous about waking the others. That meant I had to pee more often. It was a miserable night with little sleep. The next day we did our big climb up the mountain which included a section where we were tied together with ropes. I was too exhausted to complete the final leg of the climb. I didn't even have enough energy to feel disappointed in myself.

The following summer I flew to Lubeck, on the North Sea, to spend time with a German family my mother had met on the return trip of our first home leave. Anne, the Australian granddaughter, was travelling to Europe to live with her grandmother for a year. My mother arranged the holiday so I could learn to speak German. It didn't take long to discover that Lubeck's summer was on the cool side compared with the fierce Australian heat. Nevertheless, we went to the beach most days and spread our beach towels on a patch of grass. Anne's grandmother had a small wooden camp chair to sit on and she fended off the sun's rays with a wide-brimmed hat. The beach was an uninviting stretch of pebbles. For some reason I responded to a challenge to dive from the three-metre board, which I found terrifying. I completed the dive at least three times and resolved never to do it again.

We were allowed a bath once a week on Sunday and we would 'top and tail' each day with washcloths and cold water from the handbasin in the bedroom. The cool temperatures were reflected in the reserved demeanour of the family with whom I stayed.

These holidays felt like a survival test, but I did get a grounding in spoken German. I concluded from this experience that I was much more at home in the Mediterranean countries, with their seasonal warmth and their people who were loud, open and expressive in both speech and manner.

At around this time, when I was eleven or twelve, I attended a class with a male teacher who gave us a talk about respect in relationships. I clearly remember him saying in French, 'ne toucher jamais les filles même avec une plume' – 'never touch girls even with a feather'. This has stayed with me as an important life lesson. A lesson about protecting women from violence, still relevant over sixty years later.

Even as I absorbed the message of treating women with respect, I had to juggle this with the messages I was receiving at home. My father did not teach gender equality in words or in action. He openly admired women if he found them sexually attractive but did not extend this admiration to their intellect or academic achievement or to their contributions to everyday discussion. His attitude and behaviour continually reinforced my belief that women's value lay in how sexually appealing they were to men.

*With Mum at Cattolica, 1956*

*Me (right) with a friend, while on a family skiing holiday in Mittelberg, Switzerland 1958*

# Alone with my Father

At the beginning of 1959, as I turned fifteen, my mother, sister Pam and brother Philip left Geneva to travel by sea to Australia. My mother wanted to settle Pam into Women's College at Sydney University, where she was about to study medicine. I stayed in Geneva as I was preparing for my O-levels. We had moved into an apartment in Avenue William Favre, further from school than our house on Route de Chêne. The apartment had three bedrooms, a combined living/dining room, a small kitchen with a breakfast nook, bathroom and separate toilet, and a large balcony. Gilda, our Italian maid, lived downstairs in the maid's quarters. She came to the apartment each day to cook, wash and clean.

My memories of this time are very disconnected. I am sure this is because I don't want to remember. Whenever the family story of visiting Hobart was told, I would enthusiastically declare that I remembered how we had afternoon tea with family friends who lived in Hobart and then, on a drive down Mt Wellington, the brakes on our host's car failed. My sister and brother would roar with laughter, saying 'But Liz, you weren't even there.' I was certain I had been there and thought it very odd that they said otherwise. That is, until some thirty years later when I was living with my younger daughter in Canberra. It was then that I experienced a sudden realisation and moment of clarity. As I walked across the living room, I declared aloud, 'Of course you weren't in Tasmania. You were alone in Geneva with your father.'

My mother and brother were away for three months, and my father went to New York on business for six weeks over that period. I well remember that I couldn't wait for him to leave and yet I have few clear memories of the time he and I were there alone.

One memory is of accompanying my father to an evening social function. I remember the deep blue-green, shot taffeta dress I was wearing, and how the father of a classmate, a Peruvian diplomat, was ogling the decolletage of my dress. Crossing the road as we returned to our apartment, my father took me to task for what he perceived to be my flirtatious behaviour. He told me in no uncertain terms, that if I egged a man on, I was duty bound to see it through and have sex with him. I felt I was being reprimanded and broke down in tears. I hadn't been flirting with this man and I couldn't understand why my father was so angry and cold with me. My father was using this opportunity to tell me it was the man's sexual needs that mattered most. This bizarre and inappropriate lesson highlighted my father's chauvinistic attitude towards women, while leaving me confused and upset. I'm also reminded of a pattern of behaviour in which my father reduced me to tears, only to then molest me under the guise of comforting me, which is what he did.

After my mother and brother returned to Geneva, I eavesdropped on my parents. I had told my mother that my father was being sexual with me, and I wanted to hear what he said in response. I heard my father say to my mother 'She is nothing more than a selfish little bitch. You've got to face up to it Peg.' This was said about me so often by my father that I believed it. It was used to discredit anything I said.

While still alone with my father, he took me to see a Cary Grant romantic comedy and, on another occasion, to visit some work colleagues where I drank Turkish coffee for the first time. He also persuaded me to organise the large collection of loose black-and-white photos into a series of red photograph albums, for which he rewarded me with a new pair of black Bally shoes that I wanted. When in New York my father would buy Van Raalte bras and slips for my mother, my sister and me. My memory is that my underwear was mainly black and despite being of very good quality, I felt uncomfortable wearing it. I donated it, unworn, to the Salvation Army decades later during one of my house moves.

I've always had flashes of visual memory from this time – of my father's bedroom with crumpled sheets and of him half-dressed in one of his white business shirts. I don't want to take this memory further.

One of these flashbacks occurred during a medical examination for haemorrhoids at Royal Prince Alfred in Sydney during my first year at university. A memory of the white tiles in the Geneva bathroom was triggered by the white tiles in the Emergency Department I visited because of worrying rectal bleeding. I have never managed to complete this memory, but the terror I experienced at Royal Prince Alfred was as bewildering as it was overwhelming. I remember feeling completely powerless as I was examined by a young doctor. I don't remember receiving a diagnosis. Some weeks later a close friend at college, whose father was a doctor, organised a consultation for me with a Macquarie Street specialist. The difference was astonishing. Not only was I treated with great dignity and respect, but I also received a clear and reassuring diagnosis of haemorrhoids. I didn't discuss this experience of flashback with anyone. I had no idea what was happening.

I must have been on edge during the time my father was in New York on business. I was followed around town by a strange man and received some prank telephone calls at home during that time. I started believing that the two were connected and felt very nervous being alone in our apartment at night. Years later my brother told me it was a friend of his who made the calls.

# Paris

After finishing my final year and completing two A-level exams, I headed to Paris for three months. I was enrolled in a summer vacation course in French at the Sorbonne. Before the course started, I enjoyed a couple of weeks with a good friend from Ecolint and a friend of hers. The three of us explored Paris, kicked up our heels and laughed non-stop. We rented a room on the top floor of one of the wonderful old apartment buildings which are a feature of European cities. It was summer and we were in Paris. We wandered the streets of the left bank and drank coffee in the sidewalk cafes. We had a riotous evening with a group of American GIs, who escorted us home and then cruised drunkenly up and down our street, calling out our names. Everything we did had a special glow.

After my friends left, I met up with an older schoolfriend of my sister's, with whom I would spend the next three months and who was in a nominal position of chaperone while we both studied at the university. We had been booked into rather strict boarding house for women while we attended our course. My sister's friend had other plans. Conveniently, the boarding house was infested with bedbugs, which meant we had to move out. I have no memory of the bedbugs! We found cheap alternative accommodation in a little hotel in the rue du Bac and we moved into our agreed-upon separate rooms so my sister's friend could be with her boyfriend. I think this plan had been worked out well before the timely infestation. I was fine with this arrangement and happy in my tiny room which looked out onto the street. Showers were separate and cost extra, so generally I used the little basin in the room to 'top and tail'.

Early in this part of my Paris sojourn, my sister's friend, her boyfriend and I made our way to Caveau de la Huchette, only streets away, for an evening of music and dance. This jazz cellar is world famous and still operates. I'd been there, on occasion, during previous visits to Paris. Caveau de la Huchette was loud, energetic, friendly and frequented by people from all over the world. On this occasion I met a tall blonde Swede who had been in France working during the university holidays and was spending time in Paris. What followed was a whirlwind first love in my favourite city in the world. When I was having my portrait drawn in charcoal, in the little square where artists hung out in Montmartre, I learned that my blue-eyed boyfriend was engaged to a woman in Gothenburg. This gave the relationship a bitter-sweet quality which added to its intensity. We roared around Paris on his powerful motorbike, ate at little cafes, visited art galleries and savoured each moment. I missed more of my classes at the Sorbonne than I attended but still managed to pass the course, thanks to the work I had done for my A-level French exam.

The parting with my tall Swede was right out of a movie. I ran weeping along the platform, waving and calling goodbye, as his train slowly pulled out of the station.

Although my time in Paris was so special, panic managed to find me on the metro. I was in a very crowded subway carriage with people pressing up against me when I had a severe panic attack. I had to find my way out, shaking and disoriented, at the next stop. After this incident I learnt to make the trips across Paris by going one stop at a time, which was possible on the one ticket. My body was telling me something but I wasn't ready to listen.

# Return to Australia

The decision to return to Australia was the consequence of my father accepting the position of Chairman of the Public Service Board in Canberra. My sister was already studying at Sydney University and living in Women's College, and I was to join her there. I hated leaving Geneva but most of my friends were also returning to their home countries to pursue further education. I was sixteen and along with the sadness I felt an excited anticipation about the new and different life I was embarking on. A short time before we left, I met Pierre. I accompanied my parents to dinner at a restaurant with their friends, who were aunt and uncle to Pierre. He was very charming and very flirtatious, and we talked non-stop, comfortable and at ease with each other. I agreed to keep in touch by letter, never thinking for a moment we would.

My mother, brother and I spent time in London visiting my mother's relatives. I hated the dark drawing rooms and being polite to people who meant little to me. I preferred outings in London and visiting Wimpy bars to feast on hamburgers. The one exception was a visit to Reverend James Parkes and his wife, who lived out of London. James was a distant relative of my mother's and a delightful and interesting person. I knew from my mother that he had helped Jews escape Nazi Germany, through Geneva, during the Second World War. I hadn't been touched by war and this story was a source of great pride.

Finally, we boarded our ship, the *Oriana*, in Southampton. The trip to Sydney was her maiden voyage and received extensive news coverage because of her design, in particular her advanced stabilisers. The stabilisers were put to the test when we entered a fierce storm in the Bay of Biscay and were hove to until it passed. The storm created much drama as the ship, despite her size and advanced stabilisers, pitched crazily from side to side. Passengers lost their balance, and some even fell over, and the crockery and silverware just slid off the tables without a care. The excitement of the storm was followed by a calm voyage that was as enjoyable as our sea trips had always been. We arrived in Sydney and travelled down to Canberra where we lived in a rented house in Arthur Circuit in Forrest.

I filled the intervening months with holiday employment in the Department of Trade, where I compiled statistics on wheat exports to Russia and other equally strange tasks. Summer vacation jobs were plentiful at that time. My father's appointment to the position of Chairman of The Public Service Board may have helped. It was all completely new to me – government and the myriad of public service departments. I had no understanding of how government worked and yet, as I remember it, I showed no curiosity about all this newness in my life. This surprises and baffles me. It's as though a whole corner of my brain was shut down, and I just accepted whatever was put in front of me. As I always had.

I don't have strong, clear memories of those early months, but one small and seemingly unimportant fragment has always stood out. I was sitting outside on the back lawn of our rented house in Arthur Circle, with my sister, in the burning January sun, on the parched grass that substituted for lush green lawn, feeling excited by the ferocity of the heat after the temperate European summers.

For a fleeting moment my excitement translated into the thought, 'Anything is possible... anything at all.'

I finished up at the Department of Trade and prepared to move to Sydney and Women's College, where I would live while I studied for my Bachelor of Arts degree. At some stage I chose to combine it with a Diploma of Social Work, but I have no memory with whom I discussed this decision, if indeed I discussed it with anyone. It was – and remains – one of the best decisions I have ever made.

My mother and I visited an old family friend, Cecily Burton and her daughter Clare, for morning tea and discussion of what we would need to take to furnish our rooms at Women's College. Clare was also going to live in Women's College. I recall exchanging feelings of excited anticipation with Clare about this new life, even though I had no idea what shape it would take. We collected bedspreads and kettles and coffee mugs and dressing gowns and radiators, and all the paraphernalia necessary to afford some home comforts within this communal life that I had never before experienced. It was, however, second nature to some of the women in my year, as they had already attended boarding schools. The anticipation was mixed with homesickness for my life in Geneva, and in particular the intoxication and freedom of the three months studying French in Paris.

*With my brother in UK just before return to Australia end 1960*

# Women's College

Although life at Women's College was unlike anything I had known, I grew to love it for the sense of community it offered and the feeling of belonging that quickly developed. I was part of something that grew as I made friends – women with whom I am still in contact today. In my first year as a 'fresher' I shared a room with Jenny Atkins from Casino. Our room was on the first floor and opened onto a wide verandah. I was involved at the time with a boy named Robert Jordan, who would visit me at night by climbing up and over the verandah for a pash session when Jenny was asleep. Robert was dark haired, swarthy and very attractive. Our room was rudimentary – a large square with two single beds, two desks and a cupboard each for our clothes. We would put a stamp on our personal space with special belongings – a colourful bedspread, a lamp, an electric jug, a couple of coffee mugs. The jug and mugs were essentials for our get-togethers. Someone would suggest 'come and have a brew' and you'd grab your mug and packet of cigarettes, ready to socialise over a cup of coffee with other like-minded women. As time went on the groups divided into bridge players and non-bridge players. I was a non-bridge player but always ready to discuss the world's problems and the meaning of life. Socialising over coffee promoted a great sense of camaraderie. Freshers were rostered on to phone duty, which involved answering incoming phone calls and then yelling out the name, in a sing-song fashion, for the person the caller wanted. A close friend taught me to sew, and I added to my wardrobe and even made some dresses for the college dances. Many of these connections, forged in a variety of ways, developed into firm friendships which have endured through ups and downs, achievements and losses, over a lifetime.

We wore black academic gowns to formal dinner every evening and I loved the feeling of inclusion this gave me. At the end of first year, we'd unpick the seams on the sleeves of our gowns, so they were no longer joined together like bats' wings. This signified that we were now in second year and weren't required to wait on tables or perform other menial tasks.

I don't know how it started, but my friend Angela would get me to sing Burl Ives' songs and my favourite was, 'A Little Bitty Tear'. We'd sing it together and then Angela would get me to practise it. One night we wandered around the university, singing the song loudly, in unison.

> *A little bitty tear let me down*
> *Spoiled my act as a clown*
> *I had it made up not make a frown*
> *But a little bitty tear let me down*

I lived in Women's College from the beginning of 1961 until mid-1964. The college was set on an expansive block of land off Carillon Avenue in Newtown, a suburb of Sydney. It was a wonderful old building. A grand set of steps swept up to the main door which opened onto a beautiful wooden entrance hall, from which a flight of stairs circled around to the first floor of Main, as we called the building. From the front, the college boasted a covered walkway with arches, known as the cloisters, which ran almost the entire length of the building. The next two levels consisted of large bedrooms opening out onto wide verandahs, and to the right, a tall imposing structure housed a bedroom at the top of a long staircase, called Tower. I lived in Tower for my final year, because I held a position on the House Committee. Being on the House Committee (student body) was not a role that came naturally. I found any form of public office an ordeal due to the chronic anxiety I suffered.

Doreen Langley was the principal of Women's College. She was committed to advancing the careers of young women and promoting gender equality and was very much a feminist in the modern sense. She was ahead of her time. Miss Langley would invite individual students to dine with her at 'high table' when she had a guest she thought would be of interest to them.

Early on, the students in my fresher year formed into two main groups. It is fascinating to see that those same two groups, with the same group dynamics that operated nearly sixty years ago, are still evident today. This was very apparent when, in 2001 a reunion of our fresher year was organised and celebrated with a special dinner held at college. It was an exciting, heady occasion, convened over a weekend, and we naturally fell into the same groups that had existed all those years ago. We re-established old friendships and I connected unexpectedly with women I had previously regarded as too posh to befriend.

Women's College offered accommodation to students who had achieved a high academic standard. Most students came from NSW with the remainder coming from overseas and interstate. I was very friendly with a young woman who lived in Fiji and who had gone to school in New Zealand. Our point in common was that neither of us had attended school in Australia. Early on in our first year, when we both felt like outsiders, the friendship we developed helped us to feel comfortable within this community of women.

As I settled into college life, socialising and going out with men from the all-male colleges took on great importance. Despite my scepticism about staying in contact, Pierre Mongeau, the French-Canadian law student and nephew of my parents' friends, the Yalden-Thompsons, exchanged letters with me for two years after I started my course at Sydney University. The correspondence was rather one sided, with Pierre listening to my outpouring of concerns and offering sage advice. I have kept Pierre's letters, even though I lost contact with him. They hold a mirror to my first two years in college and my attempts to sort through my views on men and relationships. Pierre replied to my letters with thoughtfulness, humour and compassion.

*Tuesday, April 25, 1961*
*Avenue Victor Ruffy 23,*
*Lausanne 12, Vaud, SUISSE*
*Douce et tendre Elizabeth...*

*Don't get worried, that is simply the title of a novel I saw somewhere...Thank you for your letter and your unmerited praises on my attention to your so-called problems – if only you knew exactly how egoistic men can be and how much of a pleasure it is to talk to you, even with the "truchement" of my typewriter... scratch one illusion...!*

*My sincerest a p o l o g i e s for having understated your age and undermined your pride – it won't happen again.*

Steve: no, you had not told me his name. From what you tell me of his subsequent actions, you seem to prove my point "à rebours"! No one, love-lorn -lost or -loony, me lass, ought to act as he did with a girl, especially one who had the consideration to tell him and not simply present him with the "fait accompli" as I have often seen done, including to myself... Premièrement his attitude showed and unsuspected immaturity (and I use the word advisedly...): getting drunk in front of you was a childish way of trying to show you how he was suffering, see?... and how ashamed and pitiful you ought to be, see? what with this great martyr to the cause (trumpets, please...) of Unrequited Love (I know for I've done the exact same thing.... alas...) – then he became rude out of being at a loss, to him, Steve, out of spite and hurt pride and phoned up to boost his somewhat tattered self-respect, as he must have been feeling rather stupid. it was also an attempt to carry out his threat of dragging your name in and out of the mud. The attempt sputtered as much as he did – you are probably now acquiring the reputation of being able to "handle men... unquote... His was simply the reflex of the little boy (of any age) who kicks the door that pinched his finger. Again, I promise you that I have done the exact same things, years and years ago, as the song says...

Before I go on, I have another bone to pick with you: "... but wanted to meet a lot of people and go out with those who asked me." All of them?

*I hope you have some principle of screening them all (as I presume you don't spend your Saturday nights discussing fiscal reform with Papa...); please, mon choux: go out with those you d- - - well want to; there is no patriotic, we-must-show-the-flag-above-all bit involved! O.K.?????????????????????"*

This is an extract from one of the letters Pierre wrote, in which he responded to my musings about life in Australia, my feelings of homesickness for Geneva, my many questions about life in general and, in particular, problems I encountered in my love life. I remember going out with Steve, an older veterinary science student who lived at St Andrew's College. He became drunk and verbally abusive after I broke up with him. I had been flattered that an older student was interested in me but I soon learnt that it was more about possession than genuine interest. Once I was having coffee with him in his room at St Andrew's College – 'having coffee with' was shorthand for 'making out with' – I have a clear memory of him pushing me down on the bed and, fully clothed, climbing on top of me. I went into terror. I lashed out at him, pushing him away, and the memory stops there. I did not recognise this as a flashback at the time, but I felt increasingly uncomfortable with the way he treated me. I value how much thought and attention Pierre gave to my detailed account of the break-up with Steve. I remember it as being unsettling and confronting, and doubtless, I would have poured it out in a letter to Pierre. My father stole the last letter I received from Pierre – something I discovered after my father's death. I don't know conclusively if the missing letter had any bearing on how Pierre and I lost touch, but I strongly suspect it did. This saddens me.

A small, but for me significant, incident at college has always lingered in my mind. I went out with a friend to a party somewhere on the north shore, and we ended up joyriding in an MG sports car with one of the partygoers. We stayed out way beyond curfew. I remember being scrunched up behind the front seats as we sped up and down hills. We arrived back at college to find the principal and my sister, who was Senior Student at the time, pacing, worried and extremely angry. My sister tore strips off me, which was to be expected, and during the tirade she called me 'a little whore'. I've always wondered what was behind this name-calling. Abusive terms spoken in anger are usually reflective of something deeper.

As much as I soaked up this feeling of belonging and acceptance, the fear and panic didn't miraculously disappear. I remember fear hovering above me and dive-bombing when I attended psychology lectures held in one of the large amphitheatres. I knew to always sit on the end of a row, so I had an easy exit point. I remember holding onto the desk in front of me to stop myself from running out of the lecture. The fear of being in the limelight while fleeing would blend into the fear of staying. I also experienced panic attacks walking from college to the university. And there was another humiliating episode of mutism when I was due to give an anthropology tutorial. I had prepared the tutorial and it was written down in front of me, but when it came to delivering it, I opened my mouth and words wouldn't form. Mental health problems were not talked about in the 1960s and my memory is that the aim was to cover them up as far as was possible. Even though I was studying psychology and had chosen to specialise in psychiatric social work, I was ashamed to be suffering from some sort of mental health condition myself and I put a lot of energy into hiding the symptoms.

Because I'd learnt that my worth could be measured in terms of how men viewed me and sought me out, socialising and boyfriends were a necessary and important feature of my life at university. But the memories that matter most to me now are of the times I spent with my women friends at college… talking, laughing, being silly and being serious. I felt included in this group of young women – my peers – and embraced by them. Despite my early homesickness for the life I'd left behind in Europe, I gradually replaced it with strong bonds of friendship. The memories from this time have a warmth and simplicity and authenticity that gives them enduring value.

In the *Women's College Magazine* No 49 1963, edited by Karina Shaw and Vanessa Deans, was an entry about who I was and how I was seen by others.

ELIZABETH WHEELER
*Arts III*
*Social Work II*

*Upswept hair and "Femme" heralded Liz's entry into College. She breezed through Middle Main, the verandah presenting no great obstacle to ardent admirers. And we noticed with envy her "new look". And then came traffic in hamburgers and constant communication via the window, with increased interest in that sport called "walking" and flowers at Wesley.*

*Now, with hair swinging loose in a cloud of "Miss Dior", she tackles problems of dressmaking, letter-writing and*

*Immigration. Do we detect an orchid on the dressing table? Is her toothbrush flourished more? And isn't that shower cap fluffier? Pourquoi... c'est la vie.*

*A much-loved and malformed Teddy, an enigmatic attachment to a small blue (or was it green?) car, and our friend her sponge bag. An interest in people, a warm and understanding friend, with an infectious laugh, which is one of the most delightful things about her.*

*Très sympathique.*

# The Kitchen Knife

During the long summer holidays, I returned to Canberra and stayed with my parents in their Red Hill home. As part of the social work component of my studies, I worked for the then Department of the Interior. These 'placements', as they were called, involved several months of work experience spread across the entire course. During this time, the social work student would be closely supervised by an experienced social worker. My supervisor in Canberra, Lois Bogg, was a large woman, full of warmth, whose main passion in life was singing and performing at the Canberra repertory. She would belt out rousing songs as we drove from one home visit to another.

Home life would take me back into familiar and complex family dynamics. Mum showed her affection by cooking delicious meals which always included a traditional Sunday roast at the weekend. On one occasion, I was in the kitchen drying the dishes when my father appeared. Without saying a word, he pushed me out of the way, prioritising his need to find a clean glass for his after-lunch Corio whiskey. This small gesture of pushing me aside held all the feelings I so often sensed from him – irritation, disdain and mild contempt. Anger flooded my body and morphed into intense hot rage. A wave of red passed back and forth across my vision and my body assumed a state of readiness. I was holding a kitchen knife, and I felt an overpowering compulsion to plunge the blade deep inside him. I wanted to hurt him as he had hurt me. He was wearing a short-sleeved pale blue shirt, and his near translucent white skin revolted me. The pressure within me grew to such a degree that I was compelled to back away and move to the other side of the room, thereby creating safety for both of us through distance. My father, seemingly unaware, picked up the clean glass and rotated through the swinging door into the dining room and from there into the living-room and across to the drinks' cabinet, where he poured his whiskey. I resumed drying the dishes, feeling very shaken.

Incest survivors have every reason to feel enormous anger when they realise the extent of the betrayal inherent in the sexual abuse, especially when the abuse is perpetrated by a parent. For when the parent violates the child, they also corrupt the relationship. It took me a long time to allow the suppressed anger to surface and when it did, I didn't know what to do with it. Growing up, my father had not tolerated outward displays of anger. Consequently, it remained buried – neither expressed nor resolved. However, it didn't just disappear. As a child, I dealt with my anger by being a people-pleaser. I kept confrontation and disagreement at bay by being overly compliant.

As I grew into adulthood, I continued to avoid confrontation at all costs because I was frightened of how out of control my anger made me feel. Deep inside, I harboured a seething mass of rage that could erupt if I felt belittled or humiliated. A throwaway comment or the smallest of actions could elicit a reaction way out of proportion to what had been said or done – a sure sign the reaction belonged to events in the past.

The gesture of pushing me aside in the kitchen, as though I was a trifling irritant, triggered the rage that had been built up over the years. I was standing on a fault line and beneath my feet were layers of hurt and pain and brokenness.

# PART TWO

## Falling Apart

# The Light Switch

When I married for the first time, I was still studying for my combined Arts/Diploma of Social Work qualification. I had over six months left to complete my degree. I moved out of Women's College for the wedding, after which my husband Sandy and I rented a small flat in Birrell Street, Bondi. I travelled into the university by bus every day to attend classes.

My close friend Angela from Women's College told me she remembers a revealing conversation with Sandy at this time. Angela was working for BHP in Newcastle and would visit Sydney most weekends. She came to have dinner with us on one of those visits and recounted, while I was busy in the kitchen, that my husband had confided in her, 'every time we have sex, Liz has terrible nightmares about Fred (my father) chasing her down tunnels.' Angela was understandably at a loss about what to do with this information. In 1964 the indicators of child sexual abuse and incest were not yet known.

Part of me felt unsure about getting married but the part of me that longed to be normal ignored these flickers of uncertainty. My mother sensed something was wrong and asked if there was anything amiss sexually. If there were problems, she added, it was better to call the wedding off. Her decision to raise this was entirely unexpected because we had never discussed sex openly. I reassured her that all was well as I silently recalled how Sandy and I had enjoyed such carefree and satisfying lovemaking during our courtship. I remembered, with a smile, the many afternoons we spent in bed, in the flat Sandy was renting on New South Head Rd in Edgecliff, opposite where Abe Saffron, well-known Sydney crime figure and nightclub owner, was said to live. The flat was in one of those old red brick buildings with a window that looked out across the road. This added an extra frisson to our delicious wantonness. We were free from responsibility, family obligations and influence. Sandy was five years older than me, with a degree in agricultural science. He was very good looking and a genuine person. He had moved to Sydney to study veterinary science, which was not yet available in New Zealand. We delighted in our untroubled existence and shared great hopes for the future, but our plans didn't include the aftermath of child sexual abuse. Before our wedding I assumed our richly satisfying sex life would continue into marriage. Why would I have thought otherwise?

Sandy was in New Zealand during the lead-up to the wedding and we shared our thoughts and feelings in letters. I wrote to him and expressed concerns about many things, including whether I was ready for marriage. Sandy, always caring and thoughtful, replied with long letters addressing my disquiet and making every effort to reassure me. The real questions I should have been asking were as-yet unformed and hidden from view. I pushed aside my unease as I threw myself into wedding preparations. Because I was living in college, attending lectures and completing assignments, I coordinated the planning with my mother in Canberra.

Mme Sternberg, my mother's dressmaker, made my wedding dress. She ran her business upstairs in the Manuka Arcade. The dress was very simple, classic in style and made in an off-white Thai silk fabric. My three bridesmaids wore a soft green two-piece outfit. It was easy to get swept up in the trappings of wedding dresses, flowers and guest lists.

The day of the wedding was surreal. The ritual of getting dressed and posing for photos with my mother lacked spontaneity. Everything felt stiff and formal, and I was nervous that I would panic during the formal part of the proceedings. I rode with my father to St John's Church in Reid and when I alighted from the car and was preparing to enter the church, I started weeping, noiselessly. I slowly composed myself as I took my father's arm and proceeded to walk down the aisle. I could see Sandy looking around in anticipation. The Rev Jack Tyrrell officiated as we exchanged vows and signed the register, after which we left the church and posed for more photos. Rev Tyrell was an old grey-haired man, who epitomised my views on the clergy. He officiated at my sister Pam's wedding the year before, and my mother told me that he thought Pam was marrying a father figure.

The reception, at my parents' house, was an informal gathering with family and close friends. There were speeches and the cutting of the cake. Guests mingled and chatted and relaxed. It was a cheerful, festive occasion.

After some time exchanging small talk with friends, I changed into my fuchsia pink 'going away suit' and hat, and we left for our honeymoon in Tasmania. We drove to Melbourne and then took the car across on the ferry, so we could travel around the island. Our first stop was an overnight stay in Motel 303 just outside Yass NSW. We were greeted with two single beds instead of the double requested. I had to contrive laughter at the mistake as I inwardly faced the daunting realisation that my previous enjoyment of sex and desire had vanished. More disturbing, and completely incomprehensible, I found the thought of sex distasteful. Something had changed dramatically, and I didn't understand what or why. I was only just married and my feelings for Sandy were as strong as ever. This was no passing reaction to the excitement of the day. I knew the change was complex and deep but I put this awareness on hold.

The 1960s was not a favourable time to explore the complete turnaround I had undergone in my sexual response, let alone delve into the possible reasons for this sudden and significant change. I did, on one occasion, ask a female doctor what I could do to overcome my aversion. Her suggestion was that I have a stiff drink just before sex. I knew that this was not the answer.

It was as though the 'on' switch had turned to 'off' the moment I was legally married, and I had no idea how to turn it back on. I learnt much later that I could respond sexually when I was single and free to choose. When I did not feel I was obliged to perform. When I was in control. I had an inkling that this sexual turnoff was directly connected to the incest, but I didn't have the ability to unpick whatever process had led to this deep-seated sense that enjoyable sex within marriage was not OK. I was too ashamed, confused and afraid to initiate a conversation with Sandy about the inexplicable change in my response to intimacy. Honest communication might have made such a difference, although the child sexual abuse had muddied my understanding of love and sex, where they overlapped and where they didn't.

*My wedding day, August 1964*

*With my new husband, Sandy Ferguson*

# Five Years in Rotorua

Sandy decided we would move to Rotorua so that he could fulfil his obligation to the New Zealand government by working for a government veterinary service, and in doing so repaying the bursary he had received to study veterinary science at Sydney University. He returned to New Zealand to start work and find a house to rent while I completed my course. In May 1965 I flew to New Zealand to join him.

With the knowledge of child sexual abuse I've gained professionally and personally over the decades, and with the objectivity of hindsight, I can see patterns of disturbed behaviour surfacing during this period – patterns which continued for the next two decades, and which had a certain inevitable downward spiral about them. In the 1940s and 1950s, awareness and understanding of the long-term effects of the abuse were not yet known, which meant survivors were flying blind. I hadn't yet learnt about the harm it does to intimate relationships, nor how I would be affected so noticeably within marriage.

I was a newly married, hopeful young woman, eager to start a fresh and exhilarating phase of my life. I was pregnant and excited about the prospect of having a baby. And yet, I was remarkably naive and ill-prepared for motherhood. I thought it would all naturally come together after the birth. Having a child would create the sense of closeness and family I wanted. I wanted so much to be a good mother. I knew intuitively that the early years of a child's life were all-important but I didn't anticipate the enormous challenges I would be confronted with or my inability to meet them.

Two parts of me were vying for dominance – the unaware and hugely optimistic part, and the damaged part, which would surface regularly, seeking attention. My mood would swing from slightly manic highs to devastating and crippling lows. The birth of my second child Andrew in February 1968 brought with it great joy and, of course, additional demands as I was now the mother of two little children.

In the early years in Rotorua, I met other first-time mothers who seemed to do it all so well, leaving me feeling increasingly inadequate. Being a good housewife was highly regarded and I strived hard to achieve this so that I would be accepted. I even went so far as to bottle jars and jars of fruit, which I didn't much like and don't remember eating, but which I displayed to visitors by leaving the kitchen cupboard door slightly ajar. I made some friendships, but they lacked the depth I needed and wanted. I no longer keep in touch with friends from Rotorua, in part because of my shame about the way my life fell apart.

There were fun times when we went water skiing on the stunningly beautiful lakes nearby. Sandy owned a motorboat with his brother John, who would visit with the boat in tow, and we'd go out to the lake after work to ski. But even then, I couldn't manage these outings easily. The stress of organising these excursions seemed to outweigh the pleasure of the outing. I thought it was a deficiency on my part that I couldn't be more spontaneous.

Dinner parties were the way most people socialised in Rotorua. These were not grand affairs. A leg of lamb roasted with vegetables was common because New Zealand lamb really did live up to its reputation. This might be followed with a dessert like chocolate mousse which could be prepared in advance. Food preparation was fairly straightforward and didn't cause too much anxiety. Feeling truly at ease was harder, although we knew a few couples whom we saw regularly and who were relaxed and a lot of fun.

I remember a party at the parents' home of one of our closest friends, Liz and John Wells. John's parents, always respectfully called Mr and Mrs Wells, were part of Rotorua's upper crust. They were wealthy and lived in a large rambling house, furnished with beautiful antiques and Persian carpets, the mark of success. It was summer, leading up to Christmas. I remember the pink linen shift I wore. We took Kate, only months old, in a carry cot, in the hope she would sleep. Dinner was buffet style with chicken and ham and an appetising spread of different salads, all beautifully presented and artfully displayed on the white linen tablecloth, with plates and silver cutlery. I helped myself to a mouth-watering selection of chicken and salads, put my plate and cutlery on the tray I was given and started to walk towards where I had been sitting, chatting with some of the guests. As I walked, I must have tilted the tray just enough for my plate to slide and flip, so my whole meal landed on the Persian carpet. Overcome with mortification, I added to this social disaster, by protesting in response to Mrs Wells telling me not to worry and that she'd get me another plate, by saying, 'No, no... I can still eat it!' I started to scrape the meal, including small rug fibres stuck to the chicken, back onto the plate. Mrs Wells looked on in horror.

I developed a fear of visitors dropping in unexpectedly at the house in Jervis Street, because I couldn't keep it in magazine-like perfection, which I believed was the standard among newly married wives in Rotorua. I would hide with Kate, who was then a toddler, behind the couch in the living room if I heard footsteps coming up the front path.

Soon after I arrived in Rotorua, Sandy and I were invited to dinner at the home of one of Sandy's colleagues, whose wife was expecting a baby at the same time I was. Dorothy was a rather formidable woman both in stature and in manner, and I found myself caught up in an unspoken competition about who would give birth first and who could follow the Lemaze Vellay method of natural childbirth most closely, and declare later what a wonderful experience it was. The rivalry crept into the babies reaching milestones early and being quietly thought of as 'very advanced' which translated to 'of superior intelligence'. I found it hard to resist succumbing to this rivalry and felt it keenly after Andrew's birth. Andrew was a placid baby who was happy to engage with the world on his own terms and at his own pace. I visited Dorothy for morning tea after she too had given birth to her second child, a daughter. Andrew was slow to sit up by himself. He saw no need to hurry. Dorothy's daughter, who was the same age, was crawling with gusto and pulling herself into a seated position. Not to be outdone, I manoeuvred my good-natured son into a seated position and held tightly onto the cardigan I'd twisted firmly at the back so it would hold him in place and commented nonchalantly, that of course, he had been sitting up by himself for ages.

As a surprise, Sandy bought me a little second-hand car, so I wouldn't be confined to the house. This longed-for independence, at first so exciting, was marred when I started to have panic attacks while driving. I had no idea why I was so frightened. The fear increased the further away I was from home. And yet, if Sandy travelled to Auckland for the weekend, which he did on occasion, I would be terrified of being the only adult in the house. The terror focused on me being murdered, not on being robbed or my children being harmed. My fear was that I would be killed but I never questioned who would kill me or why. It was hard enough to get through the long dark nights. I didn't tell anyone.

I relied on medication to manage the disabling depression. Psychiatry and psychology had not yet advanced sufficiently to identify the underlying causes of these mental health conditions, which in my case, and in so many others, was childhood trauma. When I ground to a halt and could no longer function, I stayed for at least a week at my husband's aunt's home in Auckland. There I was looked after with such grace and care, and no judgement of which I was aware. But it was like putting out spot fires while ignoring the original, raging bushfire.

Although I didn't develop any real understanding of my mental health problems until the 1990s, when as a newly appointed social worker I started to learn about the wide-ranging effects of trauma, I never stopped trying to find answers for my many fears.

In Rotorua, I enrolled in an evening public speaking course. Speaking in front of an audience filled me with abject terror, something that had originated when I was reading from Shakespeare out loud to the class as a young teenager, and was suddenly rendered mute. No words would come out of my mouth. I was overcome with confusion and shame and humiliation. I enrolled in the course, determined to confront this phobia. I worked hard and practised my speeches at home and, to my astonishment, performed well. I was invited to run a course in public speaking, which struck me as hugely ironical. I declined the invitation and to this day public speaking remains a source of terror, despite that one unexpected success.

As my husband neared the end of his years of service to the government, he applied for postgraduate scholarships in veterinary science at universities in Canada and America. I painstakingly typed up the applications. He accepted an offer from Purdue University, Lafayette, Indiana, and we packed up and headed to America. I think we both hoped a new start, in a new country, would resolve the issues threatening our marriage, even though we never openly discussed it. We were struggling to fly a plane without an operating manual. A plane that was destined to crash.

*In Rotorua with my son Andrew, 1968*

# Lafayette

I still remember landing in Chicago in August 1969 and transferring to the small aircraft that took us south to Lafayette. The temperatures were unusually high, and we were kept sweltering in the little plane as we sipped lukewarm Coca Cola and waited a seemingly endless time for take-off. The intensity of the heat added an edge of excitement to this unfolding adventure.

The early months in Lafayette were exhilarating. Everything was larger than life, from the cars to the supermarkets and the widely differing accents of the American residents in the complex of duplexes where we lived. One road housed donut shops, each offering a never-ending selection of flavours. I had expected we would struggle financially but this wasn't the case. We didn't live extravagantly but we lived well. Initially, life was manageable and the rampant consumerism, after small town Rotorua, was fascinating and fun. I was still on medication, but my mood was upbeat.

I learnt to drive our large, powerful, second-hand Buick and would take my daughter to pre-school and then shop in the supermarket or visit people I'd met through my husband. I became friendly with the wife of a New Zealander my husband had known in veterinary practice. I met and visited several American families who lived in the complex, and our children played together. I tuned in to classes for a sociology course on radio and felt invigorated by the mental stimulation. We drove south to Kentucky to visit an old school friend of mine from Geneva and enjoyed a weekend playing in the snow, with the children riding on toboggans in their brightly coloured snowsuits.

Friendships began to form and they relied, to a degree, on being part of the expat community, who shared similar experiences. But there was no-one with whom I felt able to share confidences or discuss the stress I was experiencing as the shine of newness wore off. Just as in Rotorua, the fear manifested in driving. Because we lived outside Lafayette, driving was an essential part of everyday life. As the fear and hovering panic increased, my confidence plummeted, alongside my ability to cope. I was slowly and inexorably falling apart inside, while I attempted to maintain a facade that portrayed the very opposite. Eventually the facade crumbled and the old demons reasserted themselves. Mental health problems had pursued me from Rotorua, just as they would follow me back to Australia and for decades to come. Emotional breakdown was only ever one heartbeat away.

I pushed aside the enormous guilt that tormented me because I didn't want to have sex with my husband, and I didn't even begin to acknowledge that this aversion had started the very night we were married. This was in the way-too-hard basket. I wasn't ready to examine the meaning of the barely recognised knowledge that I'd enjoyed sex enormously before marriage when I was free to choose and not obligated to any man. The guilt and feeling of immense inadequacy festered and ate away at our relationship.

I don't recall any one event or a specific time that caused the original excitement and hope to morph into struggle and despair. I think it was cumulative. Little by little, the damaged part of me resurfaced and devoured the confidence I'd experienced on our arrival in America. Feeling ever more frightened much of the time, with no apparent reason, was becoming intolerable and the accompanying feelings of hopelessness permeated my life and affected my family. My husband and I decided to separate. I would return to Canberra to live with our two little children, in the belief my parents would give me the support I needed.

At this time, a close friend, Angela Cookson, now Nordlinger, from Women's College, visited Lafayette for a couple of days. I was struck by how well she seemed to be managing motherhood, with her baby in a papoose on her back. She and her husband were travelling around America. Angela arrived in Lafayette shortly before I returned to Australia. Apart from Angela's confidence with her baby, I can barely remember anything about this time, so it was intriguing and confronting when, fifty years later, Angela told me she had an account of this visit, in the form of a letter sent to her parents. She mailed it to me with permission to use whatever I wanted. What follows is Angela's impressions written at the time. They highlight my precarious emotional state and offer some brief but revealing observations relating to my father, Fred.

> *Thursday, June 4, 1970.*
>
> *[I]t was good to see Liz again, as pretty as ever but rather thin and obviously in rather a high state of nervous tension. After Bob had gone I discovered that Liz and Sandy had decided to separate for the moment anyway and she and the children were returning to Australia the following week. Apparently they have had some fairly extensive ups and downs ever since they were married six years ago and at last have decided that they must do something definite*

*instead of just hanging on and being miserable. Sandy will stay in Lafayette where he is at Purdue University doing his doctorate in Veterinary Science. The children are sweet... Kate now four and Andrew two, and the image of Liz's brother Philip. But the whole situation was very depressing and as it turned out, quite the wrong place for me to spend the four days by myself with Rachel while Bob was back at the East coast. There was another Australian girl staying with the Fergusons named Lorine Lightfoot (a girl who did Arts with Liz and has remained very friendly with her). Lorine has been slowly getting around the world and had been working in Lafayette for a couple of months. Her presence seemed to be some help to Liz but the situation was continually tense and always depressing. I stayed at a motel just down the road.*

*Friday. June 5.*

*Sandy took Kate to the zoo in Indianapolis this day and Liz seemed to calm down a bit and we spent most of the day either at her place or at the motel, chatting and remembering times past. I feel so sad that things have not worked out for her and that at this point her life is in such a mess. She is in a great state of anxiety about looking after the children by herself and for that reason has gone back to Canberra where she can be near her parents. She will however have her own flat. But that doesn't seem to be good enough as her major problem is that she has lived under the shadow of that quite strange father of hers, who has always labelled her 'beautiful but dumb', and as a result has the most all-encompassing inferiority complex and inconfidence. You may remember* some of the numerous stories about Sir Fred, that I must have told you years ago, when I knew them all well and used to stay with them in Canberra sometimes. I have not heard from Liz since she returned but perhaps will soon. I think there is little chance they will ever get together again. Sandy is a very nice guy and very easy going but he just finds Liz quite impossible to live with on a day-to-day basis and I can quite see what he means. He says he got to the point where he would wake up every morning thinking to himself 'Pray God we get through today without a drama from Liz'. She is still as sweet and kind as ever but just unable to cope with anything it seems.

Saturday. June 6.

Sandy and I took the kids to the park to relieve Liz who was not coping at all well that day. Do find myself in sympathy with Sandy's position as Liz's hysterics are very fatiguin'. Rest of the day was spent calming Liz or chatting.

Sunday. June 7.

Spent the morning looking after the Ferguson kids so that Liz could catch up on her sleep. Actually she was taking sleeping pills at the time under prescription from some doctor in Lafayette who had been trying to help her and that seemed to be adding to the general state of things. Sandy took us all for a tour of Purdue University...

Bob arrived after lunch and it was great to have him back again. He had missed Rachel more than anything else I think and was overjoyed to see his little girl again!! We then had all the Fergusons and Lorine Lightfoot over to the motel to swim with us in the motel pool. They were to stay on until dinner *but Liz got completely overwrought about the kids drowning or something and went off in a mad taking Andrew with her. Sandy and Lorine and Kate ate with us at the motel and we thrashed around Liz's problem for the thousandth time. Goodness knows if there is an answer but we all feel at the root of it is Sir Fred and he will probably only make things worse for her when she is back in Canberra. Whatever he says she think comes straight from God and he treats her as nothing.*

*Monday. June 8.*

*Called to say goodbye to Liz on our way to Chicago.*

The following week Sandy and I returned to Australia. Because of my extreme tendency to panic, I couldn't travel alone with the children. No doubt the panic was exacerbated because I was returning to seek help from my parents, although I didn't make this connection at the time. So, at vast expense, he accompanied me and our children and literally handed me over to my father who met us at Sydney airport. The significance of this symbolically is not lost on me. I can't help thinking now that I was delivered straight into the lion's den.

# Return to Canberra

When I returned to Canberra from Lafayette in June 1970, I stayed with my parents until I found a flat nearby, across the road from the Red Hill shops. It was not the mythical homecoming, with endless emotional support that I had fantasised about. My mother had never coped easily with overt emotional distress. She did her best by cooking and hanging out washing but she drank to excess in the evenings. When she drank, her conversation was repetitive. She would muse about what avenues she might have pursued had she had the opportunity, while stating, most evenings, 'Well, at least you had a happy childhood.'

My father turned predator again. I was so shell-shocked that I failed to recognise the old family patterns. Once, after I had moved into my flat, my mother screamed at me that I was self-centred, that I didn't consider her. I'd heard this so often that it fell on deaf ears.

After only a couple of months, Sandy proposed a reconciliation. He would take me on a surprise holiday to Fiji. As I look back, I'm surprised at how unwise we both were. We hadn't resolved the issues that led to our separation, and I hadn't begun to explore the reasons for my panic and bouts of depression, and occasional outbursts of rage. Not to mention my aversion to sex.

I should have had the courage to insist that I needed counselling or therapy to better manage these troubling and destructive behaviours. I took medication, which provided some relief of symptoms but offered no understanding of the root causes of these problems. Our attempt to come back together was destined to fail. The odds were stacked against the possibility of any successful – or even hopeful – outcome.

My insistence on returning to Canberra to live was a fundamental mistake borne of naive and wishful thinking. At a deep, level I wanted my family to be something it could never be. I wanted a safe, supportive healthy family, not the dysfunctional, abusive family in which I had grown up. Instead, I landed back in the same old family with its unchanged dynamics. My father didn't want my marriage breakdown and my emotional problems to make demands on him and my mother. He wanted me to be quietly compliant even as I floundered, all the time keeping up a wobbly facade of managing.

All this as he blatantly sexually molested me twice and expressed an obsessive interest in my sex life. Was he playing a power game in which he was sending out a perverse message signalling some sort of dubious sexual ownership of me? I believe so. These acts of sexual abuse were enough to keep my traumatised self in a state of chaos.

My mother sought to present a unified family front, but her needs were different. She was at a loss as to how to deal with me and my distress. She sought to placate my father about this family upheaval but then created a backlash from him by lying, claiming in a phone call with my sister Pam that she was cooking all my meals after I'd moved. He was listening in to the conversation, and forbade her to continue cooking for me, something she hadn't been doing!

When my husband suggested a reconciliation I agreed, in part as a way out of the family drama I had become the central figure in. I was made to feel responsible and I failed to recognise the all-important and devious role played by my father.

The holiday in Fiji was splendid with some memorable experiences. Our waiter at the hotel invited us to visit his home and stay overnight in his bure to eat freshly caught fish and drink kava. We were treated with warm, simple and gracious hospitality. I fell in love with the traditional songs and dance we experienced at our hotel. Over forty years later I was delighted to see them performed again on a trip with my children to celebrate my seventieth birthday. The time spent with my husband was indeed happy, with none of the stressors that lurked back in Canberra.

After we returned from Fiji, Sandy took a locum position in a veterinary practice in Young, New South Wales, a tightly knit country town where to be truly accepted took years. We lived in a ramshackle rented house, and I took the children to the local swimming pool regularly over a long hot summer we lived there. We met few people, and overall, it was a lonely time.

From Young we moved to Bowral in the Southern Highlands, where my husband worked in research at Hawthorn Park research laboratory in nearby Mittagong. We lived in a house on top of The Gib, short for Mount Gibraltar. My daughter attended Bowral Primary School. I dropped her off and picked her up and once again, driving was a nightmare. Panic dogged me on my trips up and down the winding mountain every day. It was my very own Mt Everest, and I certainly didn't conquer it.

The tension between my husband and me continued. There was little holding us together as we carefully avoided talking about the key issues that tainted our relationship. Sex, or my aversion to it, and my unpredictable moods were at the top of the list. I think I was self-destructing. I remember smashing a whole dinner set in an explosion of rage and yet I have no idea at what or to whom, the rage was directed. Nothing made sense and I felt I was going mad. What should have been the marriage of two people who cared about each other and loved their two amazing children was flailing in a sea of unknown forces. Neither of us could survive this turmoil and we separated permanently in 1972.

I went to Canberra and found a house in the newly established suburb of Curtin, for which Sandy paid the deposit. I moved there with our children. My husband continued working at the Hawthorn Park research laboratory.

As I revisit the years of my first marriage, I am taken aback at just how much Sandy sacrificed to try and save our marriage. I couldn't see it at the time. He not only spent vast amounts of money accompanying me and the children on our return to Australia from Lafayette but he also abandoned his postgraduate studies when we reconciled in Fiji. He couldn't have done more. Unfortunately, all the sacrifice, goodwill and effort in the world was not enough to resolve the underlying issue – traumatic stress caused by my father's sexual abuse.

My memories of living in Curtin with my children, are splintered. My husband's sister came to stay for a short time on her way back to Auckland from London. She was pregnant, and extremely stressed about the pregnancy and how her father in Auckland might react to it as she wasn't married. Eventually, she and the father of her child, an Englishman named John, decided to get married in Canberra, so they could return to New Zealand as a couple. My sister-in-law was some eight years younger than me and we got on well. I was in no state to support her properly, though, and the combined stress we were experiencing took a toll on us both. When they married, my mother organised chicken sandwiches and champagne for them at my parents' home. We were all pretending everything was just fine, when really it wasn't.

My children were enrolled at the Church of England Girls Grammar School in Deakin, with my son attending the on-site co-educational kindergarten. How much easier and more logical it would have been if they had gone to the local primary school. I lacked the clarity of thought, moral independence and belief in myself to contemplate this. Instead, I followed my mother's expectation that my children would attend a private school even though it made no sense for me, financially or ideologically. It highlights a blind acceptance of following what my mother wanted, even though it flew in the face of all practical, financial and, most importantly, psychological considerations. I needed to please my mother.

# The Approaching Storm

When I think back on the time with my children in the Curtin house, I have a fuzzy blank. Just as I remember what I was wearing at significant times, I remember how the house was furnished rather than what happened inside it. There was an uncomfortable, cheaply purchased brown checked lounge suite and beds from a second-hand shop. I tried to make it inviting with colourful wall hangings, and my mother gave me a sideboard and a hall table, furniture she'd inherited from her own mother. My husband supported me financially through this time.

My neighbours were outgoing and friendly, and Kate and Andrew got on well with their two children, who were of a similar age. They would all play together on the extended parkland in front of the house. This design was part of a planning scheme that offered safe, open areas, free of traffic and roads, winding all the way to the Curtin shops. Because my children attended Girls Grammar School in Deakin, I had to drive them to and from school. I was very aware that their routine and sense of security depended on my ability to make this daily drive without fuss. However, just as in Lafayette and Bowral, and even earlier in Rotorua, rising fear and panic threatened to overwhelm me when I was behind the wheel. I have never fully understood why my driving should be the target of such fear and panic unless driving represents freedom and independence and choice in both a physical and psychological sense. As I drive further away from the safety of home, I become vulnerable to rising fear and panic. There is now much greater coverage of this phobia and how it is thought to stem from a fear of losing control, which to anyone with an anxiety disorder equates to 'going mad or dying'. The only reference I have seen to a survivor of PTSD experiencing difficulty driving is John Cantwell in his riveting memoir, *Exit Wounds*. Cantwell describes how he still 'can't drive a car except for the shortest of trips into the town near our house', to which he adds, 'Bizarrely, I can ride a motorcycle without having these foolish panic attacks. I have no idea why.' Although our stories are completely different, it's oddly reassuring to know I'm not the only PTSD sufferer who has difficulty driving.

I love my children deeply and tried very hard to be the best mother I could be to them but the heavy burden of being solely responsible while mentally unwell started to take a toll. I had friends but no-one with whom I could share the inner emotional turmoil and daily horror I went through driving my children to and from school. The mundane tasks of daily living depended on my mobility and exacted a very high emotional price, which in turn cemented my feelings of failure and worthlessness. I came to dread these daily trips and yet the stability of my children depended in part on routine school attendance. It was a vicious circle. I took the Valium my doctor prescribed, but fear and panic broke through the medication and threatened to immobilise me.

On one occasion a storm broke on the way home, and I was blinded by the torrential rain. I went into panic with lightning zigzagging and thunder responding deafeningly all around me. Storms had been a source of terror for me since childhood and continue to terrify me today. I pulled over near the telephone exchange on Kent Street in Deakin, trying to reassure my children all was well as we sat huddled in my little white Mini Minor. I saw the panic and the storm through and managed to drive home. However, this episode – of which there were so many – left me physically and emotionally wrung out and despairing.

The relentless fear didn't abate, and the spiralling panic grew until one evening I went into terror so acute I felt I was staring down the barrel of complete disintegration and madness. I remember pacing around the house, distraught, not knowing what to do. What I was experiencing felt so much more intense than the usual fear I encountered every day. I had no doubt I was in the throes of complete breakdown and my very being was shattering in all directions. In desperation, I rang my husband in Mittagong asking for help. He drove to Canberra and collected the children.

They were to live with him until I was well enough to look after them again. I never did become well enough, even though I sought help and saw a psychiatrist weekly. Dr McDonald (now deceased) was a psychoanalyst who wanted to focus on my relationship with my father. I resisted, not seeing the relevance, and wanting a quick fix that would sweep away the fear, panic, depression and all the mental health problems that were preventing me from functioning normally. I'm not sure I was able to articulate this to Dr McDonald although I remember when I finished seeing him, he said he would appear in court and testify on my behalf in the event of a custody case.

I did not recover quickly. I was offered a job in the adoptions section of Department of the Interior. When it came time to start work I froze – physically and psychologically. I couldn't get there. It didn't become obvious to me until years later that working in adoptions was a crazy place to be so soon after being separated from my children.

Several months later Sandy successfully applied for a job in New Zealand. I knew nothing about this decision and only learned about the move after he had boarded the flight with my children. He flew a circuitous route to Auckland. I made all sorts of threats that I would stop him but couldn't follow them through. I think I was registering my hurt and my anger and my powerlessness in a futile sort of way. I was not in a position to do anything so, like a wounded animal, I could only let out a roar and then surrender. This was a loss I never came to terms with.

My father paid for me to see a solicitor about my legal options. I have a limited memory of what this solicitor discussed and what she proposed. It must have been much later, when my husband was firmly established in Auckland with our children, that I had to legally give him custody in order to be able see my children on access visits in Australia. I was paid $25.00 in compensation for relinquishing custody. This was an insult that hit me like a blow to my gut. I remember thinking, 'Is this how much my children are worth?'

# Loss of My Children

How do you come to terms with losing custody of your small children? Even more painful, how do you accept that you were unable to look after them? Or that you put your younger daughter at risk during the years when you drank excessively?

I don't think you do come to terms with it. The injury refuses to heal, like a deep wound whose fresh scab is knocked off when a memory intrudes or when you answer an innocent question, with a smile, that your two eldest children grew up with their father. It becomes part of your very being. You learn to deflect the pain, but it remains raw. You become practised at pretending, along with your family of origin, that it is perfectly normal for your two eldest children to live with their father in another country.

People say 'Well at least you see them now,' as though this should be enough. 'Why then does it still hurt so much,' you ask yourself.

The grief you felt, and still feel, has many layers. There's grief for the loss of the children you gave birth to, grief for your inability to parent as you would have wished, grief for your inability to freely enjoy your three children when you should have and could have. You wonder if shutting down emotionally with children is somehow related to being abused as a child. More specifically, you ask yourself whether your emotional breakdown when your eldest children were four and six relates to your own abuse at those ages. You've had a hunch this could be so, and knowing you were abused at the age of two, it is quite likely.

There are all sorts of reasons you can give yourself about why you weren't able to care for your children. They're all valid. So why don't they ease the deep hurt that you feel when you think about your son and daughter growing up away from you? Or when your younger daughter shares a memory that has no meaning for you? They really are lost years.

Then comes the cruellest realisation. Your children, for whom you wanted nothing but good, have suffered deeply for the loss of a mother and a mother who was alcoholically erratic and at times negligent, in the early years. This is almost impossible to bear, as it is forever in the past and cannot be changed, and yet the scars are apparent in the lives of those you most wanted to protect from hurt.

Now you understand how writers and poets try to put words to their indescribable pain and sorrow. The feelings that are the least likely to be told deserve to be heard too.

I lost my two eldest children to their father and the early life of my third, youngest child was marred by my alcohol addiction. This is the hardest part of my story to revisit and acknowledge as it brings up a cascade of overwhelming emotions that feel almost as painful as they did when it all happened. I feel profound grief at the loss of my two eldest children. I feel an aching sorrow and sadness that they lost a mother because she couldn't look after them. I feel unrelenting shame that my youngest child was put at risk in so many ways because of my drinking and the same profound sorrow and sadness that I was not a proper mother to her when I drank. What can I say to the three of them other than 'I am so sorry. You didn't deserve this, and I'm in awe of the adults you have become in spite of my failings.'

But from the sadness and anger and grief and despair has grown an extraordinary bond that has become a strong family unit – geographically distant but emotionally very close. It has grown through the determination of all those involved, a remarkable lack of judgement or blame, and a wish to create a family based on honesty, a deep love and connection with an absence of pretence. The wonder of this lives alongside the well of grief.

The events surrounding my mental breakdown and inability to care for Kate and Andrew are foggy. No single event tipped me over the edge. The cumulative stresses of being solely responsible for the children while being overwhelmed by unacknowledged feelings linked to the sexual abuse certainly contributed.

That evening, when I rang Sandy and told him I couldn't look after the children, I was in a state of agitated terror, believing I was losing my grip on reality. I felt I was about to fragment into a myriad of little pieces that could never be mended and made whole again.

My memory is that Sandy drove to Canberra and picked up our children and took them back to Mittagong with him. At a later time, we agreed verbally that this arrangement would be until I was able to care for Kate and Andrew again. I don't remember any of the practical details like packing up clothes or saying goodbye or explaining what was happening.

What I do know is that, without my knowledge, Sandy took our children to live permanently, 2,000 kilometres away, in Auckland, New Zealand.

# Access Visits

My partner, and second husband-to-be, Tony, drove me to the airport to meet Kate and Andrew when they arrived in Canberra for their first access visit. Because they were unaccompanied minors, the air hostess walked with them from the aircraft to where I was waiting. Canberra airport was very small back then. After lots of big hugs, we collected the luggage and piled into the car for the drive home to Curtin. I kept my feelings contained even though my heart was bursting. I felt complete once again. I sat in the front passenger seat with my body turned around to face Kate and Andrew, as we chatted about anything and everything while I sought to reconnect with them. Andrew looked up at me with a big grin on his face, his eyes alight. He pointed to the long-sleeved, blue patterned shirt I was wearing and stated triumphantly, 'Helen has a shirt just the same as yours.' I felt as though I had been punched in the gut and my joy in the moment collapsed against my will. And yet Andrew's face remains etched in my mind and my heart as he looked at me with such delight and hope at his discovery. He had found a real and tangible connection between his mother and his father's new wife.

I have no idea how the timing of access visits was arrived at. I remember being *told* when Kate and Andrew would visit. I was still unbelievably distressed that Sandy had taken my children to New Zealand. That hurt would have manifested in extreme anger. I contacted one of his aunts when I was drunk and lashed out verbally. I was treated as of no consequence when a few years later, at a Christmas gathering at my father's home in Red Hill, my sister told me the next access visit had been cancelled as Andrew had been more asthmatic than usual after the previous visit. The message was delivered in an offhand manner with the whole family listening in. I was stunned into silence, unable to absorb let alone react to this news.

Visits took place approximately every twelve months and my children would be with me for two or three weeks. The anticipation leading up to the visit was intense and my emotions were all over the place. Excitement was the overarching feeling, but it was accompanied with bursts of fear which stemmed from my history of not coping. In the early years, my children looked so young and vulnerable when they arrived. My joy and love were always framed with sadness when I saw them walking towards me.

It wasn't all smooth sailing. How could it be when twelve months were squeezed into three weeks with none of the usual reference points like school and friends or regular activities and familiar living arrangements? For Kate and Andrew, access was like a mini holiday. Any hazy connections to a previous life in Canberra had been replaced by their new life in New Zealand. I resisted this reality, and I didn't help bridge this divide by asking about their lives in Auckland. In addition, my seething resentment towards their father and his new wife prevented me from seeing my own glaring failings as the non-custodial parent.

My mother was still alive during the first visit and she took them up to the cafe on the top of Red Hill for an oversized gelato. This had been something of a ritual when Kate and Andrew lived with me in Canberra. They both have warm memories of her as a caring grandmother who took them to different places in her little red Mini Minor. She took us all to the Cotter Reserve, where Kate and Andrew played on swings and climbing frames and we had afternoon tea in the little cafe.

I have many photos of the visits and it's good to be reminded that there were happy times despite the length of time between visits. Kate and Andrew bonded easily and naturally with Emma after her birth in 1975. Andrew and Kate would carry Emma around the house, pointing things out and teaching their little sister about the world.

In the early access visits Kate looks serious and guarded in most of the photos, whereas Andrew has a more open and energetic involvement in whatever was happening around him. When they were with other children, they were both understandably more relaxed and able to enjoy whatever they were doing. I think the separation was enormously difficult for them and I wasn't nearly sensitive enough to this. When they came for Christmas, I was able to concentrate on all the traditional festivities like a tree and decorations and choosing presents. It gave us all something known and familiar. I would choose their presents carefully, wanting to give something that they could enjoy that would remind them of their time with me.

Sometimes it all became too much and I fell into a heap. This occurred on one Christmas access visit. The build-up, combined with Christmas, was a bridge too far, and I retreated to my bedroom, unable to deal with any of it. I used to think if I could just have a short sleep, that when I woke, I'd be on top of things. It never worked. I couldn't nap – I was way too keyed up and hypervigilant. I would take Valium and wash it down with wine... a disastrous combination and a pattern I repeated often. On this occasion I hadn't even wrapped the presents. On this Christmas Eve, Kate and Andrew realised I wasn't going to reappear, so they hunted around for where I'd hidden their gifts and set about wrapping them themselves. I was relieved to discover many years later that they had found this unusual reversal of roles different and exciting. I felt a complete failure.

Just as there was the build-up and excitement with Kate and Andrew arriving so, too, there was the anguish of departures. After one visit, just before I was about to start a new part-time job, Tony had recently had surgery and had come home from hospital with a large supply of Di-gesic for the post-operative pain. Packets were left strewn on the chest of drawers. I was feeling so low and miserable after Kate and Andrew returned to Auckland that one evening before bed, I started taking the pain killers. I was almost robotic as I swallowed one after the other and 'just another one' in an attempt to deaden the pain. I then went to bed and slept. In the morning, as I got ready for my first day in my new job, and I sat on the edge of the bed drinking my coffee, I observed my hands growing larger and then smaller and then larger and smaller again. From what seemed a great distance, I realised I was hallucinating. Somehow, I made it through my first day.

Despite the heavy feelings attached to each visit, the contact formed a foundation on which we could build a relationship. This does not belie the deep hurt inflicted on all three of my children as a result of this rupture in their relationships with both me, their mother, and with each other. The pain continued to burn for many years.

*Access visit in Curtin*

*I felt time running out from the moment Kate and Andrew arrived*

# Alcohol Abuse

Alcohol was part of everyday life when I was growing up. When a visitor was greeted with 'What are you drinking?' it referred to alcohol, not tea or coffee. It was only when I returned to my parents' home as an adult, when Sandy and I were trying to work out whether we could save our marriage, that I became aware of my mother drinking to excess. I was embarrassed and ashamed by how she was affected by alcohol in the evening but true to the unspoken Wheeler rule, we would all pretend it wasn't happening. I didn't recognise that my mother was in all likelihood, trying to convey her disappointment about not pursuing early dreams, and regrets that she hadn't achieved more. My father drank consistently and at regular intervals through the day but did not show the effects in his speech or manner. Once, he raised his glass to me and declared, 'This is my Valium.'

I wasn't attracted to alcohol in my twenties. I found it a bit scary. I was terrified of losing control, so I drank socially but not to excess except on one notable occasion. In second year at college, a good friend and I bought a flagon of cheap red wine and went and sat on St Andrew's College oval and drank it. We became very drunk and later had to sign in with the night porter on our return to college. We thought we'd hidden our drunkenness superbly but were violently ill when we reached our rooms.

I didn't drink much during the following years. It wasn't until I moved in with friends at Swinger Hill in the early 1970s that I began to drink heavily. This was in the months after my children had gone to live with their father and my friends suggested I live with them rather than live alone in an empty house. I felt safe and supported at Swinger Hill, which was a factor in letting go and drinking. Later, when I returned to my house in Curtin, alone and without my children, I continued to drink heavily as a means of self-medicating. It didn't take long for alcohol to become a problem. The warmth of the cask wine coursing through my body quietened the fear. A by-product was that I felt more confident and capable, not unlike my mother with her empty dreams. The big mistake I made was mixing alcohol with antidepressants and sedatives. I didn't know that it would increase the effects of the medication, although I doubt it would have mattered as I became more and more addicted to the feelings that alcohol gave me – a world of peace and tranquillity in which I could do whatever I wanted.

During the months at Swinger Hill I made considerable progress. I obtained a position as Employment Officer at the then Canberra College of Advanced Education. This gave me the opportunity to brush up my administrative and organisational skills. Because I worked as part of the Student Counselling Centre, my interest in psychology was revived through discussions I had with one of the psychologists. I enjoyed working with students from many diverse backgrounds at the college. I also met my second husband, Tony.

After I moved back into my house at Curtin, Tony moved in and I became pregnant with my younger daughter, who was born in February 1975. For a period, there was some stability and structure in my life although for months after my daughter's birth

I suffered what can only have been severe postnatal depression (PND) which manifested as the most terrifying thought that I was going to harm my baby by drowning her every time I gave her a bath. I can still feel the relief I experienced each time I delivered her to safety after rinsing the soap off her little body.

The marriage didn't survive the constrictions of my mental health problems and my husband's change of career and move from the Commonwealth Public Service into the private sector in Sydney. I couldn't envisage living in Sydney with a small child while coping with daily panic and the overwhelming stress of my limited mobility. I stayed in Canberra and Tony moved to Sydney alone.

As I absorbed the failure of my second marriage and the feeling that something was very wrong with me, I started drinking to deaden the self-loathing and failure. Alcohol took over insidiously and my judgement became increasingly impaired. Socially, I would often drink to blackout point and then would come the need to phone a trusted friend and piece together how I had behaved the previous evening. There were times when I remembered just enough detail to feel overwhelmed with shame and humiliation the next morning. I was told by a friend who witnessed my journey into alcoholism that I would always rail against my father at the end of an evening. I didn't ask her exactly what I said but I gather it was a repetitive and predictable refrain.

Twice In the 1970s I was admitted to a psychiatric ward after I had overdosed on Valium and drunk large quantities of alcohol. The first time I was admitted to M ward at Royal Canberra Hospital and the second time, for a longer period of two or three weeks, to the psychiatric ward at Calvary hospital. I was under the care of a psychiatrist on both occasions but have no memory of any therapy. I overdosed on two other occasions but discharged myself from hospital after twenty-four hours.

One of these short hospital admissions occurred when my brother and former sister-in-law returned to Canberra after some years in the UK and gave me two very attractive little tops for Kate and Andrew purchased in Kathmandu. I thought, as I thanked them, 'how am I supposed to give these to my children? They don't live with me.' I left the welcome home dinner at my parents' house, went out and slept with an occasional lover and overdosed. As I recall, my brother took me to hospital. My family regarded my actions as attention-seeking.

Because I drank to excess for over a decade, memory of what happened at significant events is fractured. My father held a party in his home for our joint seventieth and fortieth birthdays just before the actual date in January 1984. There were several very old family friends present, one of whom said to me, bitingly but with a smile, 'I didn't bring your present because I didn't know whether you would turn up.' This comment hit a raw nerve. It highlighted everything that I couldn't do and for which I felt both guilty and judged. At the same time, it lit a fuse of submerged anger about the lack of understanding shown to me by my family of origin and their friends.

I was so angry. I drank, trying to soothe the fury surging through my body. I refused to go home with my then partner and daughter. Instead, I stayed and drank and confronted my father about his sexual abuse. I have no idea what I said or what he replied, only that he put me in a taxi and sent me home. I ended up in the wrong driveway, fell and skinned my knees and ripped my dress. My daughter told me later she thought I'd had a physical fight with my partner.

I made many attempts to stop drinking. I attended Alcoholics Anonymous briefly but had a disagreement with my sponsor, who insisted I give up all prescribed medication as well as alcohol. I flatly refused, and we parted ways.

My rock bottom came when I gave my eight-year-old daughter a leg-up to get into my next-door-neighbour's house so she could open the back door and allow me to steal a bottle of vodka. (I did replace it!) I drank the whole bottle and then went cold turkey on 12 January 1984. I haven't had a drink since. Going cold turkey was stupid and dangerous. A friend sat with me through the awful days of withdrawal, and I took Valium regularly for the indescribable feelings of terror. I was frightened I would have the DTs, about which I knew little, and which I understood were terrifying. They epitomised being completely out of control. After about two weeks I was through the worst and ready to live alcohol-free. My life didn't miraculously heal itself, but I was one step closer to understanding what had gone so horribly wrong. And why.

# The Parties at No. 9

My only direct contact with the Canberra scene was through my father's 'No. 9' parties at his home in Red Hill. He held these Christmas parties every year, in early December. He invited friends from over the years and whichever family could attend. They started at 6pm and would continue well into the evening with a group of hard-core stayers.

Guests were ushered into the living room as they arrived and as the numbers grew, they spilled into the generous front entrance or the dining room, and occasionally into the kitchen on the other side of a swinging door. A feature of these gatherings was a never-ending supply of alcohol and my father's alacrity in topping up, or refilling an empty glass, while he said a few complimentary words to the guest. He circulated and spoke with everyone. He was a smooth and accomplished host.

The living area was spacious with the light-coloured carpet my mother had selected when she redecorated the house. The room was furnished with a teak sideboard, a nest of black coffee tables, a large three-seater sofa and an assortment of lounge chairs covered in different shades of green. It was a comfortable and inviting room but not grand. During the parties the furniture was adjusted to open up the space, although a large round, tan-coloured table was always left in the centre of the room to accommodate glasses, ashtrays, handbags and other items. Once the guests reached that magic number, and shyness had been eased with alcohol, the chatter increased and became louder, and the sharp bursts of laughter became more frequent. The bar was set up on the extended dining table in the adjacent dining room with the hired glasses in neat rows, bottles of alcohol, soft drinks, jugs of water and buckets of ice. My father planned everything in meticulous detail. Additional ice was stored in the laundry tub.

The food was catered, which meant there were always platters of finger foods to be served to guests. This gave me an excuse to break away from the cocktail conversations and make my way through the crowd with a smile on my face and a large plate of neatly presented asparagus rolls. My parents' friends were well meaning. They enquired after my health and asked what I was doing, but my standard reply about community needs and health centres failed to ignite a lively conversation.

In the early years I enjoyed attending the annual Christmas do. It gave me an excuse to buy a new outfit at The Camel Train in Woden and I enjoyed looking good. My presence at the party was largely decorative and that was how I felt. When I was still drinking, the sharp outlines were softened, and I felt able to greet people and have superficial conversations. After I gave up drinking, these occasions opened up a raft of deep, uncomfortable feelings and I had a strong sense of not belonging. In those years I was becoming much more aware of the effects of the abuse. I felt both angry and a hypocrite.

As the years passed, I wanted to withdraw from my father, even though I wasn't sure how to do this. I found the parties hard work rather than a pleasure. I was always expected to attend, and on one occasion, I remember my father literally shoving me forcefully into place at the front door to welcome guests. I could feel my resistance growing. I didn't know the guests beyond a passing acquaintance and then only because I was a Wheeler. I had no interest in mingling with the Canberra crowd. I'd never been part of the scene and had no wish to join it. I was the only Wheeler child living in Canberra, and, at that time, I was the least informed about what was happening politically. I was too busy trying to survive.

There was a period when quite a few of my brother Philip's old ANU friends came along and brought with them a more relaxed attitude and energetic exuberance. Or perhaps it was a generational thing. Judy Rossiter, with her curly hair and expressive eyes that were quick to fill with laughter, was there on one occasion. She had returned to Canberra with her daughter after her husband's death and I saw a lot of her. Judy was non-judgemental, supremely honest and very vivacious. We had a lot in common, talked easily and laughed a great deal. On this occasion, we were sharing stories of how, when we flew into a rage with our former husbands, we would remove our wedding rings and hurl them onto nearby parkland, as some sort of dramatic statement. We both remembered spending hours searching through grass, dirt and stones to find the lost rings once we had calmed down. As we shared this coincidence our laughter grew louder, verging on mild hysteria. Guests nearby, looked on in bewilderment at both the story and the hilarity that accompanied it.

During one of the parties, when Kate and Andrew were over from New Zealand and Andrew was barely a teenager, he discovered there were no rules or supervision, and he helped himself to cans of Fosters from the fridge. Much later he told me that on returning to New Zealand, he went to the fridge and reached out for a beer – only to be confronted by his stepmother, who witnessed this in shock and told him under no circumstances could he just go and help himself to a beer! It spoke of the 'free for all' atmosphere inherent in these parties. Meanwhile, Emma and her cousin Vic would watch videos in my father's bedroom, and help themselves to Kit Kats and dry ginger ale, which left Emma feeling quite ill for want of a decent meal.

Despite the humorous stories, the parties at No. 9 did reflect my attempt – and eventual success – in moving beyond my father's control. It took a very long time, but I wrote to him before his last party in 1993 saying I would not be attending ever again.

# My Third Husband

I met my third husband, Yaroslav Andreas Mamchak (Andrew), at a small social occasion. At the time, I was employed as Welfare Officer at the Woden Senior Citizens Club, and I was feeling my way back into normality after a lengthy period of severe agoraphobia when I was pretty much confined to home. I threw myself headlong into the job. After some months, I met husband number three. I had grown enough in confidence that I probably appeared to be a together person but the past still cast a long shadow. I remember engaging with Andrew at our first meeting over his master's thesis about postwar reconstruction in Australia, and my father's prominent role in it. By the end of the evening, I had agreed to meet up with him again. He suggested taking my dog for a walk, which seemed benign. There wasn't a strong physical attraction on my part, but Andrew had a self-assured manner and I responded to that. He had big bushy eyebrows, like Robert Menzies, and a fascinating background. His mother fled Ukraine with him as a baby towards the end of the Second World War. I was always attracted to connections with Europe.

That first meeting had to be cancelled because my daughter Emma was involved in a horse-riding accident. It was a Saturday, and I went into work that day as I had arranged, with a friend, to put on a fashion parade at the Senior Citizens Club for members and friends. My friend Jenny owned Christina Fashions in Curtin and her clothing range included fashion suitable for mature women. Many hours went into getting everything ready. On the day, Jenny introduced the clothes while behind the scenes I organised the sequence of garments being shown by the volunteer models. I also modelled some of the dresses. At first I was nervous parading in front of the guests but after a short time I found a sort of rhythm and confidence and really enjoyed it. Then, unexpectedly, I received a phone call from the teenager with whom my daughter Emma had gone horse riding, to say there had been an accident. I quickly handed over my role in the fashion parade to someone else and drove back home.

Emma was in a great deal of pain and appeared to have broken the elbow on her right arm. I put her carefully in the back seat of the car with her arm propped up on a folded blanket and we drove straight to casualty at Woden Hospital. I drove as smoothly as possible, but Emma cried in pain when we hit even the smallest bump. I talked to her in what I hoped was a soothing and reassuring manner.

After arriving at casualty, the medical team took over and Emma was taken for X-rays and assessment. Eventually, one of the doctors on duty appeared alongside me in the soulless little cubicle where I was waiting. He explained that given the complexity of the break, Emma would require surgery but whether it would be performed that day depended on a number of factors. Emma would need to be transferred to the paediatric ward at Royal Canberra Hospital and the timing of surgery was significant in terms of the type of pain relief that could be administered. On one level, I absorbed the information. On another level I felt completely overwhelmed. The tears started and wouldn't stop. I felt so completely alone. The doctor let me cry and cry and conveyed a depth of caring and understanding beyond words. I remember looking at the cold, hard white floor of casualty and thinking 'I just want to lie down and curl up into a foetal position and stay there forever'. I so wished there was someone there to support me.

Practicalities took over. Emma was transferred by ambulance to Royal Canberra Hospital. Once it was established that the orthopaedic surgeon on call would not operate until the next day, she was given pethidine for the pain. The change in my daughter was startling. She became contrite about the harsh words she had spoken in response to the extreme pain and morphed into this expansively loving child. I soaked up the change and eventually felt able to return home to shower and eat something and prepare for the next day and the surgery.

Back at home, the feelings of isolation and helplessness rose up again. I felt tired and completely wrung out. I was at this low point when Andrew Mamchak rang to see how I was. I latched onto his offer of support as I gabbled on about Emma and the accident and the pain and casualty and the surgery. Andrew listened, quietly offering comfort through his presence. We agreed to put our 'dog walking' expedition on hold and Andrew said he would contact me after Emma's surgery. This small commitment gave me hope and softened the feelings I had been battling.

The feelings of complete aloneness that I experienced in casualty didn't evaporate as my relationship with Andrew progressed. They just went underground, continuing to have a profound effect on my behaviour. I concocted a scenario in which I was part of a family that was warm and nurturing and always supportive. I wrote a script and enacted it and placed Andrew

Mamchak at the centre. Having both been previously married, we each had children who grew up separately from one another. We were families with complex backgrounds and on the surface there appeared to be strong similarities. We continued to see each other and Andrew later told me I put pressure on him to marry. I think he was right. I even stage-managed the perfect wedding, set on the lawns of the National Botanic Gardens, attended by friends, my father and his friend Wilma before a reception at his house. Of the utmost importance to me was that my father 'gave me away' in the old tradition of marriage. I didn't understand the underlying meaning of this request at the time, just as I couldn't see that Andrew didn't offer a warm supportive environment. He was verbally abusive with Emma and critical of my son Andrew. He was also harsh and blaming about my aversion to sex after we were married. We had little in common. He would get intensely annoyed when I stayed late at work. He even raised the question of finances in the event that I was 'invalided' out of the public service and insisted I demand Emma's father increase the child support which meant I had to ask my sister for the money to pay my solicitor. When we separated, he fought for every cent he could, even though he brought only debt into the marriage. I had duped myself with an illusion of what I thought would fill that achingly empty part of me.

# The Gynaecologist

At Andrew Mamchak's insistence, I attempted to overcome my block about sex in marriage by making an appointment with a Sydney gynaecologist who was reputed to be a specialist in helping women overcome sexual problems. We drove to Sydney and stayed with a close friend from my Sydney University social work days. She and her husband were very welcoming and warmly hospitable. I did not approach the medical appointment with an open heart and mind. I knew this 'freezing' was psychological in origin and deep down I must have known that it was bound up in the concept of marriage and belonging to another person, and the sexual abuse by my father. I didn't know how to untangle the elements which I intuitively knew to be the cause.

The appointment was a disaster. The doctor took a history, but the only treatment he recommended was to learn about my body through masturbation and to read the popular self-help book *Everywoman*. I saw an explosion of red across my field of vision. I reached out and swept everything off the doctor's desk onto the floor and stormed out. To this day, I don't know whether I only imagined my response or actually carried it out! Then I burst into tears. I found the attitude of this 'specialist' arrogant, patronising and completely lacking in sensitivity and insight.

Through years of reflection, it has become clear that my understanding of relationships and my own sexuality were irreparably damaged at the hands of my father. The secrecy surrounding the acts of abuse led to feelings of intense shame and the shame secured my silence. This allowed my father to maintain his power over me.

In her book *Father–Daughter Incest*, Judith Herman states,

> But from a psychological point of view, especially from the child's point of view, the sexual motivation of the contact, and the fact that it must be kept secret, are far more significant than the exact nature of the act itself. From the moment that the father initiates the child into activities which serve the father's sexual needs, and which must be hidden from others, the bond between parent and child is corrupted.

I don't think Herman's powerful observation is confined to fathers and daughters. I believe wherever secrecy and the exploitation of power are at play, the honesty of that relationship will be permanently affected.

As a young married adult, I was approached by the husband of a good friend at a social gathering who made a sexually suggestive comment while we danced around the living room with carefree abandon to reggae music. I found the comment both shocking and offensive and yet I did not call it out.

On another occasion, an older man who was not known well to me, brushed his hand over my breasts with complete nonchalance. This furtive action was undeniably sexual in nature, and it took place so quickly that I wondered if I had only imagined it. I knew I hadn't as the feeling of violation told me it was real. We were in a crowded pub at the time, a place where such acts are often overlooked and almost never called out. But this is no excuse. Alcohol does not perform the action.

Common to every experience of this nature was a recognition that the offending man believed he had every right to behave this way. Consent was never considered. These incidents left a memory that forever tainted my association with the male person in question and the unspoken code of silence dissuaded me from even talking about it with close female friends.

I experienced the other side of the power dynamic when I was married for the second time and I behaved very seductively with a married man I met at a party. I was inebriated and arranged to meet him for a liaison some days later. Fortunately, events intervened, and the liaison didn't happen. I can remember the feelings of intense shame that crept into my being once the effects of the alcohol had worn off and the equally intoxicating feeling of complete power had dissipated.

As an adult I'm aware of the indescribable confusion I must have felt during the sexual acts perpetrated by my father. In addition, the confusion was intensified a million-fold, because I remember feeling intense physical pleasure as I was being abused as a small child, and this was followed by an all-over feeling of terrible shame, which I didn't understand. As an adolescent, I found the tongue kisses repellent and the way my father would stick his tongue in my ear intolerably intimate. These sexual behaviours, and his many throwaway sexual comments, prevented the development of a normal father–daughter relationship. Instead, it was a relationship built on confusion, fear and dread and one in which my father exploited his control over me. It's no wonder that each time I entered into a new marriage and signed the register, this implied contractual control would change something inside me. I also never learned how to foster intimacy through sharing experiences, deepening friendship and common interests.

The anger I felt towards the gynaecologist, arrogant and insensitive though he was, masked a deep and furious rage at my father for pursuing his perverted sexual needs. I now understand this deprived me, his daughter, of an opportunity for close and healthy relationships.

# Symbiotic Learning

I'm not sure what I expected to gain from counselling, nor can I remember clearly just what I did achieve. I know I wanted to eradicate the relentless feeling of hopelessness as I tried to juggle unremitting fear and bouts of depression while maintaining an outward appearance of normality and coping. In the 1960s and 1970s I succumbed to the shame attached to mental illness, believing deep down that my mental health problems were the result of innate weakness and 'just not trying hard enough'. This internal conflict originated in part from my father's intolerance of emotional displays and his rejection of all things psychological, which kept me from recognising how the sexual abuse had impacted me so extensively. He was derisive of my chosen profession of social work and seemed only to value careers which involved administration or management. I felt great internal conflict as a result and like most adult survivors, I struggled with believing what I did remember about the abuse, an all-too-familiar dilemma most child sexual abuse survivors face as adults.

I started my quest to find answers in earnest in the 1980s, when events combined to open my eyes to the way in which the effects of childhood sexual abuse carried into adulthood, often in a very disabling way, much like the after-effects felt by Vietnam veterans. Along with increased knowledge and understanding, change was beginning to occur in the ways women who experienced sexual violence were viewed. Women who worked in women's services endeavoured to expand their response to meet the needs of adult survivors. I was in both camps: a survivor wanting to learn all I could about this connection and a social worker wanting to offer counselling that was informed by the latest research and knowledge available.

An important step in my recovery was when I successfully applied for a job as Welfare Officer at the Woden Senior Citizens Club. The club was only ten minutes from my house in Curtin, and the part-time hours fitted in with my daughter's schooling. I believed I had the knowledge and skills to establish this newly created position. I spent the next three and a half years developing the job and introducing new and well received activities to the club.

There, I started a monthly newsletter, *The Meridian*, which featured contributions from club members, information for senior citizens, and a program of monthly activities. I introduced and facilitated a writers' group, which proved a popular means for club members to tell their stories. We put on a musical play, written and directed by a local playwright, which injected an amazing energy and vibrancy into the club. My social work background meant that I could offer informal counselling, make referrals and serve as an advocate in matters such as housing. I was intensely proud of my achievements in this position. The downside was that I didn't keep to my part-time hours, and often took work home with me. My need to do a job well has always taken precedence over work–life balance and I've never learnt to manage the two properly. As a result I got very close to burnout. I knew it was time to leave.

When I resigned from the Senior Citizens' Club, I was farewelled with a sumptuous afternoon tea and gifts and speeches.

Because the farewell lasted through my final work afternoon, I returned over the weekend to tidy up the office and sort through the files and information in readiness for my successor. Late on the afternoon of the Sunday, as I was finishing up and had rung home to tell my daughter that I would be leaving very soon, I was violently assaulted. An intruder had come in through the top window of the room next to the main office where I was working. I had opened the window to air out the smoke from my cigarettes.

I have a fleeting visual memory of a man in a light-coloured jacket and then I go blank. I managed to reconstruct the assault from the trail of blood in the club and the injuries to my body. My handbag was found some distance away from the club minus the cash I had withdrawn not long before. The large pool of blood on the floor in the club, combined with the cut to my right temple and bruising in the shape of fingertips behind my left ear, strongly suggested that my head had been bashed on the metal strip that secured the carpet at the edge of the parquet floor in the main hall. I checked my underwear for any sign of sexual assault when I got home and was relieved there was none. Even though I couldn't consciously remember what had happened, my body held the memories. For approximately three months after the assault, I had all the symptoms of acute post-traumatic stress, which was nothing new. Really, it was a composite of what I had experienced over the previous thirty odd years but in a more condensed, acute and disabling form. I was extremely fearful all the time, jumpy and unable to drive outside the familiarity and safety of my own suburb of Curtin. I had great difficulty falling asleep and an inability to concentrate.

I was referred to Dr Maxine Tennant, psychiatrist, at Phillip Health Centre, for treatment. I saw Dr Tennant on a regular basis. She told me I was suffering from retrograde amnesia and during one of our sessions she asked me, seemingly out of left field, 'Were you abused as a child?' I cannot remember the context, but I do recall being startled by the question. When I look back, my reaction to the mugging was no different to the symptoms I had been exhibiting much of my adult life. These same symptoms were magnified after the assault at the club. Perhaps this is why Dr Tennant asked me about childhood sexual abuse. Whatever the reason, I found this question enormously affirming, and it temporarily quietened the self-doubt that I often experienced. It was the most meaningful interaction I remember from those sessions, and it freed me up to talk about what I did remember of the abuse.

As it turned out, there was also an upside to the assault...

While confined once again, I noticed an ad in the *Canberra Times* for a job as a part-time locum social worker. The position was in a southside suburb which I could imagine being within my scope of attainment geographically, if I put in the necessary work and practice. With this in mind, I applied for the position and was shortlisted for interview. The interview was to be held in Kambah. Although only about five kilometres from my home, at that time Kambah was for me the equivalent of travelling to the other side of the planet. Somehow, I made it to the interview and because I was so amazed and elated by my achievement, I think I must have presented with absolute confidence as well as answering the standard questions satisfactorily. I was offered the position at Narrabundah Health Centre.

The experience I'd had working with Dr Tennant gave me useful insights and a deeper appreciation of the value of counselling that I could take with me to my new job at Narrabundah. I job-shared with another part-time social worker and learnt more about the position during our overlap time, when we discussed cases and alerted the other person to any possible action that might be necessary on behalf of a client. The model for community health at that time was based on a multidisciplinary approach and we worked closely with allied health professionals. The disciplines included physiotherapy, nutrition and community nursing, and were supported by the two medical practitioners employed by the Health Department. In addition, there was a long-time private doctor who rented rooms at the health centre and who made referrals to the social worker and other professionals. Narrabundah Health Centre was friendly, always busy, and a focal point in the community.

My social work job was initially a locum position which eventually became permanent. It coincided with large numbers of survivors seeking the same affirmation I had found with Dr Tennant, as they too sought to tell their stories and be heard, believed and supported. Because the number of social workers in the community was small and the demand for counselling high, community social workers undertook peer training and we shared resources amongst ourselves. I volunteered to do a presentation on 'adult indicators of child sexual abuse'. As I researched material for the presentation and recorded my findings, I realised I could tick almost all the boxes. It was unnerving and yet strangely validating.

During my years working at Narrabundah, I privately engaged in bodywork with two therapists. This was centred on deep massage in tight areas of the body that were judged to be holding onto trauma and interfering with freedom of movement. The aim was to encourage the patient to let go of past suffering. On occasions there could be profound shifts at a mental level as well. I so wanted this to work because I agree with the findings that our bodies store memories of trauma. I sought to be free from the crippling fear that plagued me. I wanted the frequent awfulness of falling into the black abyss to stop. But it didn't.

I left Narrabundah to work full time at Phillip Health Centre for a year. This backfired when I had a stress breakdown and went on sick leave for some weeks. The tipping point was running a group for survivors of incest with a colleague from Women's Health Service. We had successfully co-facilitated two groups for women experiencing depression and, because so many women were victim-survivors, we decided to run a group for incest survivors. It was glaringly obvious that this would cause stress overload… and it did. I have a brief but vivid memory of my daughter Emma driving me to an appointment with my doctor, Suzanne Davey at her southside Kambah practice. I was in no state to drive myself. Even with Emma driving, I had this overwhelming fear that I would open the car door and throw myself out. A strange but terrifying compulsion. Suzanne responded calmly to my distress and prescribed a period of sick leave with review appointments to monitor my progress. She also adjusted my medication and suggested that working full time was probably not realistic. She was right. I worked part time up until my retirement in 2010.

I continued my roller-coaster ride of 'not yet diagnosed' post-traumatic stress disorder during the 1990s and began regular therapy sessions with psychologist Lynne Geary. I think of this therapy with Lynne as offering a holding place. I've always viewed my recovery from incest as an ongoing process and not one that is ever complete. A comment Lynne made has stayed with me and offered me a small degree of comfort when I'm overwhelmed with grief and shame at how badly I let down my children when they were little. I was telling her how much this haunted me, and Lynne observed, 'You showed them change is possible.' She was referring to how I had given up alcohol.

In the mid-1990s when I was preparing to travel to New Zealand for my eldest daughter Kate's wedding, Lynne, through careful questioning and observations, helped me recognise that my fear of flying had its origins in the abuse by my father. She uncovered the pattern of the terror I experienced and how it was at its very worst when I was flying towards my father in Canberra and how by contrast, it diminished markedly on the trips away from him. Insights of this kind are of no use to the client if they are delivered on a platter. They must be gently revealed to the client, so the client has ownership of the insight. Lynne helped me to understand a great deal about my abuse and, in addition, she taught me techniques for grounding myself when I was in flashback. I trusted her and valued her skill as a counsellor.

There is no guarantee that consulting a therapist will afford a positive experience. I saw a psychologist who claimed to have expertise in trauma work and all I can remember of that short-lived encounter is that she raved on about the wonderful relationship she had with her husband. To me, a three-times married and three-times divorced woman, hearing about her 'wonderful marriage' accentuated my own feelings of inadequacy. It destroyed a relationship that never began. My faith in counselling was restored when, sometime later, I connected with Jane, a psychologist who listened intently and had a gentle empathy, and with whom I felt able to share my feelings. Quite early on in in our contact I remember crying for almost a whole session as her perceptive questions opened up the grief I needed to acknowledge and feel. I also told her of my intention to write my story. I look forward to personally delivering a copy of this memoir to her.

Every bit as important as the professional counselling were the informal, yet invaluable, conversations I had with a colleague who became a very good friend. We worked closely together when I job-shared with Marie for a period at Narrabundah Health Centre and I regarded her work very highly. Our friendship has continued and deepened since then. Marie was one of the first friends to whom I disclosed my father's abuse. She also was my support person at my father's funeral. She has listened to me at times of crisis and when things were on a more even keel. Marie has the rare ability to listen fully and completely, without judgement, and her responses and insights are always thoughtful and perceptive. Marie has offered me unconditional support alongside her wisdom and experience. She has been a major figure in my journey of understanding, and I am deeply grateful. It's rare to have a friend who can offer this degree and depth of support. I have been very fortunate.

My personal experience of therapy over many decades with psychiatrists, psychologists and social workers is that it's not the number of degrees that determine how effective a therapist is. It's their ability to listen wholly, with the wisdom to know when to ask questions that allow the client to explore additional, deeper but relevant threads of their story. I've consistently been guided by the statement I learnt in social work lectures almost sixty years ago: 'always start with where the client is.'

I've also learnt much from professionals in this field such as Gabor Maté. I became familiar with him and his work when I watched his documentary *The Wisdom of Trauma* in 2020. Maté looks at the high incidence of trauma and the way it manifests across society in the form of mental illness and addictions. He sees it as the root cause of many incarcerations in the prison system. The film is compelling viewing. Maté, a Hungarian-born Canadian doctor, specialised in addiction and trauma. He doesn't believe addiction has a genetic basis and his approach can be summed up when he says, 'not why the addiction but why the pain.' His approach uses a powerful technique he calls Compassionate Inquiry which helps the client to recognise the unconscious dynamics that run their lives. And it sums up what I think I was looking for when I threw myself into different therapies, looking for answers.

# Silencing

It was the summer of 1992–93, and my younger daughter and I were living in a small rented house in the inner southern suburb of Lyons. This followed an emotionally tumultuous year of separation from my third husband and the lengthy process of negotiating a property settlement. I had been granted sick leave in November the previous year as I struggled with an emotional breakdown.

I was still on leave on 9 January 1993, the day of my father's and my joint birthdays. As had been the tradition for many years, my father rang to wish me a happy birthday. I started to reply with the usual platitudes while, in my head, I wrestled with the hypocrisy of these empty words. I remember feeling angry with myself for buying into this absurd pretence. Pulling myself together, I took a deep breath and confronted him once again about the abuse. I told him I wanted him to take responsibility for the incest. Even though my body shook uncontrollably, and tears poured down my cheeks, my voice held steady and firm. There was a deathly silence either side of a long pause, at the end of which my father said in his usual, slow precise manner, 'A figment of your imagination, my dear.'

Sometime later, seemingly out of the blue, I was swept up into an ever-intensifying vortex of terror. I flashed back to a time in my childhood and what must have been a threat by my father if ever I told. All I could hear was the menacing utterance that 'a hitman will come and kill you.' I didn't question the truth of this threat. Deep inside, folded in the layers of memory, the child I once was believed this to be true. As the terror escalated, tightening its grip still further, I reached out and phoned my good friend Marie and asked her to come over. She must have heard the urgency in my voice as she arrived soon after my call. She knew of my history of abuse and she didn't question the degree of terror. We sat outside on the grass in front of the house. She offered me unquestioning safety and support, while slowly I returned to the present moment. It felt like an endless afternoon, but time can stretch and warp in these moments.

Flashbacks are often explained using the analogy of grandma's scones. If you unexpectedly come across the delicious smell of warm, freshly baked scones wafting out of the open front door of that little white house you pass on the way to the bus stop, it might take you back to a much earlier time, when as a child you were in your grandmother's kitchen. With abuse flashbacks the same thing is happening, but the memories elicited are not bathed in a warm nostalgic glow. Through whichever sense the memory is experienced, it is likely to be full of fear and the content is almost impossible to believe, such as my father's threat to have me killed if I disclosed the abuse. Far from being an exaggeration or overreaction, it is entirely consistent with the kind of threats reported by adult survivors.

# Taking Control

When I returned to work at Narrabundah Health Centre in 1993, it felt like coming home. It turned out to be a very important move. I don't think anyone had anticipated the number of adult survivors of child sexual abuse who would emerge from the community, wanting to disclose and tell their stories, as the prevalence of abuse and incest became known in the 1970s. We were offered additional training for working with survivors and we would share our knowledge at the regular monthly meetings for community social workers. It was at one of these social work meetings that Chris Staniforth, head of Legal Aid in Canberra, came to give a talk about what legal aid was all about and who was eligible to seek help from the organisation. I remember Chris saying that the service had advocated for survivors of sexual abuse on occasion. I tucked that information into my head to mull over.

By this time, I had confronted my father three times on the phone, asking him to acknowledge the abuse. Like so many survivors, in my mind it was of the utmost importance that he admit the truth of what happened. I couldn't accept his continual denial and insistence that I had imagined the abuse. I simply wanted him to say, 'Yes, it happened.' I knew it had, and his denial amounted to him calling me a liar. Like so many survivors, I had examined the truth of my memories again and again. Perhaps I naively thought that an acknowledgement would sweep away the decades of damage, fear, depression, self-loathing and relationship problems I had endured. I was obsessed with the idea of an admission by my father, never anticipating the fallout that would accompany it.

After much thought and feeling terribly nervous, I rang Legal Aid and made an appointment to see Chris Staniforth. I remember very little of the two-hour meeting with him other than I cried a lot and Chris was most generous with his time in the supportive space he created. I told Chris my story, and his skilled and patient questioning prompted discussion of the damages I sustained. Chris and I agreed that he would send my father a letter with the allegations of incest and the resulting damage. Not long after the interview, Chris sent me a draft copy of the letter, which I read carefully and corrected, and a final copy dated 13 July 1993 was sent as agreed. I include a copy of this letter, with my father's annotations, and a copy of his response, dated 6 August, in which he denies any truth in my allegations.

At the time of sending the Legal Aid letter – and in the months before – I had ceased contact with my father. I wrote him a short letter saying I wouldn't be going to his annual Christmas party in December 1993 and other than his letter denying the incest, we had no contact. His eightieth birthday and my fiftieth rolled around on 9 January the following year. I received a big bunch of native flowers from my sister and brother but I don't remember any birthday wishes from my family of origin. I do remember feeling very flat and empty, but I also accepted that it was I who was responsible for a seismic event in the family, by sending the Legal Aid letter. Something I had no regrets about.

It would not be until after his death that I discovered how my father had intentionally drawn my sister and brother and their partners into being party to his denial of my allegations.

# LEGAL AID OFFICE (A.C.T.)

North Building, London Circuit Canberra ACT 2601   Telephone (06) 243 3411   DX 5638   Facsimile (06) 247 5446

Our Ref:   CJS:KEL

cc: Saw
    Plf
    Nefi
    (AS)
    Koltz

3 copies per

Rec'd
5/7/93

13 July 1993

**Personal and Confidential**
Sir Frederick Wheeler
9 Charlotte Street
RED HILL ACT 2603

Dear Sir Frederick

## CLAIM BY YOUR DAUGHTER, MS LIZ MAMCHAK

We have been consulted by Ms Mamchak. She has sought legal advice from us regarding a claim for compensation in respect of personal injuries which she has, in general terms, detailed to us.

She instructs us that from the time she was about 5 years old until she was 28 years old you committed acts upon her which may well be found to be wrongful acts of incest. She indicates that she has suffered loss as a result of those acts, namely:

- medical conditions including alcoholism for 10 years, Valium addiction for 20 years, ongoing anti-depressant medication since the age of 20 years, and diagnosis as suffering manic depression, sexual dysfunction resulting in the breakdown of 3 marriages, agoraphobia - first panic attack age 9 years - condition still current.

- hospitalisation after overdoses -
  Calvary, 3 weeks
  Royal Canberra Hospital, between 2-3 weeks
  Royal Canberra Hospital, two overnight admissions
  Woden Valley Hospital, stomach pump
  (at least one other incident of overdose not requiring hospitalisation);

- breakdown, December 1992, requiring four weeks unpaid sick leave;

---

Address all mail to: CHIEF EXECUTIVE OFFICER   GPO BOX 512 CANBERRA ACT 2801

Chief Executive Officer
O.J. Staniforth B.A. (Hons) LL.B

Assistant Executive Officer
K.M. Fryar B.A. (A.S.) (Hons) LL.B

*12 copies per [handwritten]*

- loss of income and professional advancement including being only able to work part time until May 1993, often in menial positions with geographic restrictions;
- inability to travel, outside Australia, outside the ACT and inside the ACT, without substantial support;
- relinquishing custody of the children Kate and Andrew in 1973.

Ms Mamchak now seeks compensation for that loss. While she finds the loss she has suffered immeasurable in dollar terms, she is seeking from you a nominal amount of $25,000 which will allow you to acknowledge to her the wrong in your behaviour.

The sum sought, we are instructed, does not equal the purely financial loss incurred by Ms Mamchak as a result of her injuries. Accordingly you may find her request that of a reasonable and honest person seeking substantive acknowledgment of prior wrong behaviour rather than a person seeking to profit from you.

We are instructed to request that you respond to Ms Mamchak directly in writing to her address, 43 Gruner Street, Weston ACT 2611.

Yours sincerely


C J Staniforth
Chief Executive Officer

# FREEHILL
# HOLLINGDALE
# & PAGE

6 August 1993

Ms L Mamchak
43 Gruner Street
WESTON ACT 2611

Dear Ms Mamchak

**CLAIM AGAINST YOUR FATHER**

We are acting on behalf of your father, Sir Frederick Wheeler, who has given us a letter sent to him on your behalf by the Legal Aid Office (ACT). The letter requests Sir Frederick to respond directly to you in respect of the matters raised and he has instructed us to reply on his behalf.

Your father is distressed at the allegations that you have made to the Legal Aid office about him. Your father denies that there is any truth in them.

It follows from your father's complete denial of the allegations that he rejects your claim for compensation.

Notwithstanding the above, your father wishes you to know he is willing to resume normal family relations at any time should you so wish.

Yours sincerely

*Freehill Hollingdale and Page*

FREEHILL HOLLINGDALE & PAGE

# Above the Clouds

During a phone conversation, my eldest daughter Kate asked me bluntly whether I would come to New Zealand for her funeral if she died. I was taken aback by the question but it made me think about what I would do were such an event to occur. I had concluded that overseas travel was too far outside my comfort zone. Kate's question shook me and made me think.

Reality came soon enough when Kate told me she and her partner Mike had decided to get married. This news was cause for great excitement and my absolute need to work out how I would get to Auckland for the wedding. I looked into the possibility of travelling by ship but there wasn't an easy way, and it would take valuable time. I realised I would need to confront the sheer terror I felt when trapped in an aircraft for over three hours.

I hadn't been in a plane for over twenty-five years and my memories of air travel were horrific. My phobia had begun when I lived in Rotorua in the 1960s and made the trip to Canberra with my two little children alone, while Sandy recovered from tonsilitis. On that occasion I was sucked into a state of abject terror as we taxied down the runway preparing for take-off. I asked for the aircraft to be turned around so I could be dropped off at the terminal. Such was the degree of my fear, I couldn't understand why this was not possible. I continued the journey in a fog of disorientation and somehow made it to Canberra. One of the few supports I could lean on was a new prescription of Valium. During my visit, I had nightmares about flying and having to choose which child to save when the passenger window next to me blew out. My mother contacted Roland Wilson, both a friend and the Chairman of Qantas, to ask how the air crew would deal with me if I freaked out completely. The answer was that I would be placed in a straitjacket, which to someone whose terror originated from feeling trapped added another layer of dread.

And yet I had loved flying as a child and feeling the thrill of immense power during take-off. I remember a flight at the age of ten or eleven when I flew to Lubeck on the North Sea in Germany, where I was to stay with a family for some weeks to learn German. The plane was a small DC3. We entered an almighty storm and the plane was tossed about in the sky as we flew through it. I thought it was enormously exciting and I loved every moment as the plane pitched back and forth. As I learnt much later in counselling, the terror I experienced years later was directly related to the abuse and was psychological in origin.

My doctor, Suzanne Davey, told me about Fearless Fliers, a program run by Qantas, for people like me who were too terrified to board a plane. I contacted Fearless Fliers and, after being interviewed for suitability for the program, signed up for the next course. I felt equal measures fear and excitement. There were talks by Qantas engineers about how the aircraft worked and learning how to identify the different sounds the engine makes on take-off and landing, as well as all the safety measures. A psychologist taught the group relaxation sequences, and we learnt different techniques that would help us to keep focused on the reason we were travelling by plane. For me that was a series of cards with statements written in black Texta reminding me I was going to see Kate and Andrew and attend Kate's wedding. I also tried to visualise being involved with the wedding preparations, which included Emma, my younger daughter, being fitted for her bridesmaid's dress.

But first I had to complete my maiden voyage and graduate from Fearless Fliers. The plan for that momentous day started with a flight to Sydney, after which we would visit the Rocks. We would then all have lunch at Coogee Bay Hotel. Late afternoon, we would board the flight back to Canberra.

The day started very early as we gathered in nervous excitement at Canberra airport. Then time seemed to accelerate as we boarded our flight to Sydney to embark on the full day's activity. I remember wandering around the variety of stalls at the markets at the Rocks with a sense of wonderment. I might as well have been on a pioneering trip to the moon such was my sense of achievement. Late afternoon arrived all too swiftly, and when we boarded our flight home there was a sense of triumph that was on the verge of exploding like a brilliant fireworks display. At Canberra airport we disembarked and farewelled one-other with effusive congratulatory messages. I finally stood at the top of the stairs at Canberra airport, feeling as though I could take on the whole world and all its problems. I was high on adrenaline and the feeling was euphoric. Emma was waiting for me at the bottom of the stairs, and she looked up at me, her face full of questions. I could read 'How did it go?' in her eyes. My proudly victorious grin was unmistakable.

Emma and I travelled to New Zealand together in 1997 for Kate's wedding and we shared the uniqueness of everything associated with this adventure. Emma got to have my free allocation of drinks on the plane and when we arrived Kate and Andrew were at the Arrivals section waiting to greet us. We travelled to Northcote Point where Andrew had a little flat that he had vacated so we could stay there. It had a wonderfully tranquil vibe. After our arrival, we spent time chatting and catching up and learning about what was planned for the days leading up to the big event. It felt so good to all be together, sharing details of organised events which also included my nephew's wedding on Waiheke, a popular little island in Auckland's stunning Hauraki Gulf. Of the significant events planned, the one I dreaded was meeting Helen, Sandy's wife, and reconnecting with Sandy after so many years. They had invited us for lunch at a restaurant at the waterfront before we all boarded the ferry that would take us to Waiheke for my nephew's wedding. Any detail of the lunch is lost in a haze, apart from the memory of sweat trickling cold and wet from my hairline down my neck and back as we exchanged pleasantries over lunch. I also remember Helen asking Sandy if she could borrow his reading glasses to see the menu. This small detail told me my first husband and his second wife shared a comfortable intimacy. It was not something I had ever experienced and unlikely I ever would. A momentary flash of envy passed through me.

Kate's wedding was held in a church in Remuera and was picture perfect. I wasn't sure where I fitted in. Sandy and Helen were clearly running the show and I didn't want to create any waves. I remained in the background as much as possible but Emma, in her forthright manner, made sure I was in all the appropriate photos and Andrew offered me his arm as we exited the church.

Both these gestures made me feel included. At the reception, a former boyfriend of Kate's, who had come with Kate for a visit to my house in Curtin many years before, insisted I get up and dance with him, another thoughtful and warm recognition of my place as 'biological mother of the bride'. Mike, Kate's new husband, acknowledged my efforts to physically get to the wedding which I very much appreciated. These attentive and caring acts made all the difference to what could have been an awkward situation in which I felt like a shag on a rock. My sister and brother-in-law, who were in New Zealand for their eldest son's wedding, were also in attendance. I said hello to them when they were seated at their table at the reception, but we didn't have any further contact.

Kate and Mike's wedding was the first of many trips I would make to New Zealand to spend time with Kate and Andrew and my granddaughter Claudia, after her birth in January 1998. I averaged an annual visit until Covid halted trans-Tasman travel.

This trip to New Zealand was a major turning point in my recovery. I had broken through the constrictions of fear that left me unable to fly with a very similar program to the one that had freed me from being held captive in my home. Both these disabilities were a result of the sexual abuse. To be able to travel again was liberating and wonderfully exciting and heralded a major step in my healing journey.

# PART THREE

## Fragments

# Father Joe

With the advent of the internet and dating sites, I became a regular user. With the wisdom of hindsight, I think my real aim was to discover how men viewed incest survivors. I was conducting my own research project. I had a burning need to know if men looked down on sexual abuse survivors or regarded them as 'used goods' or were turned on at the thought of children being sexually abused.

I met a range of men, had some very funny experiences and suffered from hurt pride when I was dumped. One of the more unusual incidents involved a very presentable man with whom I had coffee a few times and eventually dinner. I thought he had potential as a partner. He was interesting, a good conversationalist and attractive. He openly told me he was seeing several women and finding it hard to choose who to concentrate on. Finally, after a very enjoyable dinner, he announced that he had chosen someone else but he wanted to gift me a book. The book, which he said had spoken to him in a profound way, was *Father Joe* by Tony Hendra. I was so angry I never read it.

I was working at Tuggeranong Health Centre at the time. One day, several weeks later, I had a new client, an attractive woman who wanted to talk about relationship problems. An important relationship had recently ended, and she wanted to understand what had gone wrong. She was distressed and tearful. As she described the man involved, I started to think, 'this sounds eerily familiar'. She had met him on the internet, had seen him a number of times and thought there was a real possibility this could develop into something serious. When she told me he was seeing a couple of other women with whom he also had a strong connection, I started to feel decidedly uncomfortable. However, I listened intently and empathised when appropriate. She went on to tell me he had finally chosen one of the other women with whom to pursue a relationship, but he wanted to give her a copy of a book that had really spoken to him.

The book was *Father Joe* by Tony Hendra.

* * *

Many years later, I retrieved the book from its dusty corner in my bookcase and decided to find out what it was all about. I was curious to know why he had chosen to give a copy to at least two women he had dated so briefly. *Father Joe* is the story of a deeply troubled young man who seeks salvation from Father Joe, a gentle, wise, and very human priest with whom he forms a lifelong bond.

Did he see himself as a saviour of wounded souls? Or was this his way of revealing he too was damaged from past experiences? What message was he sending, and why?

# The Twilight Zone

Over the years I filled endless exercise books with my thoughts and observations and used journalling as an attempt to purge feelings of fear, that often morphed into terror, and which persisted day after day, week after week. As I re-read the journals, I am struck by how relentless these feelings were and how I had no means of dealing with them. It is only now that I have learned more about emotional flashback that I realise that this is what was happening for me.

In my journal entries I recognise that my terror is about past events. In May 1997 I try and explore what might have caused such intense feelings, asking 'what might have made me so terrified that I became almost paralysed with fear?' Some years earlier, in November 1992, I wrote:

> *Hell*
> *Drowning ... down, down, down*
> *Hell is*
> *Remembering*
> *Reliving*
> *And above all feeling those long*
> *repressed feelings of a child in*
> *terror, pain and confusion*
> *No-one to turn to*
> *No-one there*
> *The depth of sadness and grief*
> *Is almost more unbearable than*
> *the abuse itself.*

I was regularly having nightmares. They started when I was living in Canberra as a child. I dreamt I was being chased, in the dark, along a street of cobblestones between tall buildings. The only escape I had was to take off and fly through the dark, narrow street, always knowing that death would result if I was caught. After struggling to become airborne, it would be the fear that kept me aloft. This nightmare recurred over the years, changing only in location. The last one I remember was set in Germany in the Second World War. I was chased by uniformed Nazis across green fields, over hills and through trees to an old castle. When I reached the castle, I ran up and down narrow, stone corridors through a rabbit warren of passages with the Nazis getting closer and closer as my terror grew. These dreams resulted in me being literally frozen in fright and the feelings would follow me into my waking hours.

My mother told me I would sleepwalk as a child, and she spoke of the time I was seen 'wafting up the driveway of our Canberra house.' On another occasion I'm told I sleep-walked into the room I shared with my sister, pushing her friend, who was staying for the night, out of the bed and into the crevice between the bed and the wall. These anecdotes were always told with much laughter. The sleepwalking stopped after moving to Geneva but was replaced in adulthood with episodes of sleep paralysis in which I felt sure I was awake, but I was unable to move any part of my body. Experiencing this paralysis was terrifying and I would imagine I could somehow throw my body onto the floor to force some sort of movement.

Other disturbing dreams and nightmares I recorded in my journals were more wide-ranging and featured my father and siblings and, on occasion, my mother. The themes were very much around sexual assault, rape and being alone, ostracised by family and being followed by unknown men in the dark. It was always dark. These dreams were intense, disturbing and menacing. In one, I woke not knowing where I was and became terrified as I searched for clues that would give me an answer. I used grounding techniques to bring me back into the present and where I was once again living – in my house in Canberra. In consultation with my counsellor, I referred to this state, between sleep and waking, as the twilight zone. Because the feelings threatened to incapacitate me, I learnt to introduce movement in the form of energetic dancing to ABBA in my kitchen first thing in the morning. This really did help transition from a state of past terror to being in the here and now. I kept up the dancing routine for years and still find it one of the best ways to ground myself.

Re-reading the decades of journal entries, for the first time since writing them, offers revelation into how I was held captive by the effects of the incest. It's no wonder so many survivors of early childhood sexual abuse believe they are going mad when they are caught in this no-man's-land of intense fear and terror for no apparent reason. Bessel van der Kolk has a section on flashback, dissociation and reliving in his book, *The Body Keeps the Score*. He writes:

> *Dissociation is the essence of trauma. The overwhelming experience is split off and fragmented, so that the emotions, sounds, images, thoughts and physical sensations related to the trauma take on a life of their own. The sensory fragments of memory intrude into the present, where they are literally*

> *relived. As long as the trauma is not resolved, the stress hormones that the body secretes to protect itself keep circulating, and the defensive movements and emotional responses keep getting replayed. ... however, many people may not be aware of the connection between their "crazy" feelings and reactions and the traumatic events that are being replayed.*

He also writes, 'Flashbacks and reliving are in some ways worse than the trauma itself', something I recognised and wrote about in my journal entry in my poem 'Hell'.

It took a long time to make sense of my chaotic inner life. Understanding the cause and effect of child sexual abuse came about slowly and in a piecemeal fashion, with occasional 'ah-ha' moments. One of these moments occurred after I started my job at Narrabundah Health Centre in 1989. As community social workers, we would share resources we found helpful for our clients, which is how I came to read *Toxic Parents* by American psychotherapist Susan Forward. *Toxic Parents* is an easy-to-read book which uses many case studies to explore dysfunctional families. The chapter on incest, 'The Ultimate Betrayal', resonated with me. Forward writes:

> *Many people are shocked when I say that the incest victims I've worked with are usually the healthiest members of their families. After all, the victim usually has the symptoms – self-blame, depression, destructive behaviours, sexual problems, suicide attempts, substance abuse – while the rest of the family often seems outwardly healthy.*
>
> *But despite this, it is usually the victim who ultimately*

*has the clearest vision of the truth. She was forced to sacrifice herself to cover up the craziness and the stress in the family system. All her life she was the bearer of the family secret. She lived with tremendous emotional pain in order to protect the myth of the good family. But because of all this pain and conflict, the victim is usually the first to seek help. Her parents, on the other hand, will almost always refuse to let go of their denials and defences. They refuse to deal with reality.*

*With treatment, most victims are able to reclaim their dignity and their power. Recognizing a problem and seeking help is a sign not only of health but of courage.*

When I read this passage, I remember thinking that it reflected the truth of my situation. It not only gave me hope, but it also validated my own experiences. It was like someone saying to me, 'I hear what you are saying, and I believe you.'

# Memories Told in Flashback

In recent decades research has shown how memories of trauma are stored differently from memories of everyday life. Different parts of the brain are involved, as seen on MRI imaging, for implicit (trauma) memory and explicit (everyday) memory. As Bessel van der Kolk says in *The Body Keeps the Score*:

> *As a result, the imprints of traumatic experience are organised not as coherent logical narratives, but in fragmented sensory and emotional traces: images, sounds, and physical sensations.*

This can be confusing for the trauma survivor who will struggle to make sense of the fragments, which are not experienced as a complete narrative with a beginning, middle and end. I can attest to this, as I have experienced flashbacks (implicit memory) during my adult life that were so intense they transported me to another time in my life, but which I didn't recognise as flashback at the time, nor could I place them within a complete memory as there were no visual components with which to form a narrative.

In 1988 my sister and her husband invited me to a gathering to celebrate their twenty-fifth wedding anniversary at their home in Clareville in Sydney's Northern Beaches. By then I was almost five years sober and married for the third time. My husband decided to make an occasion of it. He hired a larger, more comfortable car than his small Holden Gemini and booked himself, my daughter and me into a hotel in Manly with a room on the tenth floor with sweeping ocean views. He was given to grand gestures. We drove from Canberra to the hotel where we showered, changed and made our way to the party. We must have been a little late, as all the other guests appeared to be there. My sister had invited mostly family members with a few old friends of hers and her husband. There was, as I remember, a vast and delicious array of food, lots of alcohol and lively greetings and chatter and laughter either side of a couple of speeches. My father was there, seated at a round table, whisky in hand as he managed and directed the conversation around him. As the elder of the Wheeler family, he was treated with special respect. He was in his element, and he was in charge.

My fourteen-year-old daughter mingled with her cousins. I chatted with family members, finding the gathering, as always, something of an ordeal. I was told, 'you scrub up well' by my former sister-in-law as I moved around in my purple pantsuit. I wore it because it gave me an outer feeling of confidence. As I no longer drank, I couldn't use alcohol as a crutch, but I drew on the social skills I'd learned decades before as a teenager. I don't recall talking to my father, but I do remember the way his presence permeated the occasion, as it always did. I could sense him in the crowded, noisy room even though I didn't seek him out. I felt alert and vigilant.

After the party, we returned to the hotel where the three of us shared a large room with a sitting area and sliding doors out onto the balcony. Fear of heights was but one of the many phobias I suffered from. I couldn't sleep, and as time went by, I was overwhelmed by wave after wave of terror and the belief that if I did go to sleep, I would sleepwalk out onto the balcony and jump. The blackness of the night stoked the fear which kept me upright in the chair. My mission was now to keep myself awake through the interminable hours ahead to ensure that I stayed alive. It was a waking nightmare. I sat and smoked cigarette after cigarette as I willed the night to end. When the morning came and the terror faded with the dark, I was able to sleep. We booked the room for another half day so I could catch up on some rest. I was, however, emotionally wrung out when we finally packed up and set off for Canberra mid-afternoon. By the time we reached Lake George it was night once again, and with it came further paralysing terror. Lake George had always seemed sinister to me after the drowning of some Duntroon cadets many years before. In the dark, even as a passenger, it was unbearably frightening and took me to a place of frozen terror. We stayed overnight in a motel in Goulburn and completed the journey the next day, when it was light, and the terror had lost its hold. I didn't recognise it at the time, but I had been in the grips of a long and exhausting revisiting of a past emotional state.

After I found my way back into my career as a social worker, I was enjoying a dinner at the Southern Cross Club with two social work colleagues who had become good friends. It was just an evening out, sharing a meal and enjoying the conversation of friends with similar interests and views, when an incident occurred nearby in the club. My memory is that two uniformed policemen arrived at the club, not far from where we were sitting, to evict a male customer who was drunk and abusive. A scuffle ensued. When one of the policemen held the man down on the floor, with his arm twisted behind his back, I went into flashback. I froze and went into terror. The scene I was witnessing triggered some deeply traumatic memory. My friends were very caring and concerned and I remember one of them asked me if I had been raped by a policeman at the time of my DUI, years before, when I was waiting for my father to collect me. My answer was a definite 'no'. I don't know what memory I had flashed back to but my fear was overwhelming and extreme.

Sometime later, when I was working full time and co-facilitating a group for women who had experienced incest, with a colleague, I pushed myself in a way that had unexpected consequences, largely because I didn't know how to care for myself as an incest survivor. It was a very stressful time with my third marriage breaking down and an acrimonious separation. A much-repeated pattern was unfolding, the upshot of which was emotional breakdown. Again.

This is what I recorded in my journal:

> *Flashback in social work interview prior to 'break-down' in Lyons in Dec. when I am interviewing a known client and talking about her plans or actuality of running dance school for school children and I move out of my body; a flash of me in black leotards and tights as I used to wear when I did ballet in Geneva. I am stunned and very scared at being out of my body and on the ceiling and struggle to return while I am interviewing this without her knowing. This was I think the week I went off on S/L and had what seemed like weeks of living in sheer terror. I felt incredibly, horribly alone. My daughter got me to doctors appts and I recall that being absolutely terrifying. I lost masses of weight and think/feared being anorexic as well. I remember being too frightened to sleep for fear of what I would see.*

This memory was of the time I took ballet classes in Geneva. I'd always loved ballet and fantasised about being a prima ballerina, dancing effortlessly and with unbelievable grace across the stage. It was the image of my developing body in tights and leotard that triggered this intense, out-of-body flashback. Our classes were held in a large studio with one entire wall built from mirrors, so the dancers could critique their work. I was not among this group of advanced dancers. I was in the beginners' class where we worked largely with floor exercises. When I saw my developing body reflected in these vast mirrors, I was terribly unsettled. The image contributed to my giving up my ballet classes. I was ten going on eleven.

A visual image of me in a cot, wearing tan covered overalls, has always played on the outer fringes of my memory. I am about two and a half years old and I am in the living room of the house in Durville Crescent. It's winter and there's a fire burning in the fireplace. My mother is very ill with the measles and she, my older sister and I sleep in the living room where it's warm. The image of me in the tan overalls has appeared from time to time during my adult years and I have always dismissed it with a shrug.

Then, in the year 2000, I visited my eldest daughter and my two-year-old granddaughter in Auckland, as I now did most years. My daughter was going through the painful process of separating from her first husband. I was sleeping in the living room where she had made up a bed for me. There was a fireplace in the living room. My granddaughter was wonderfully outgoing and confident, and I enjoyed helping my daughter look after her. When my granddaughter needed her nappy changed, she would lie down on the floor and wait for the nappy change to happen, then run off to continue playing. I also supervised her in the bath where I talked to her, sang to her and washed her. She was comfortable and completely trusting with me.

One night I fell asleep in the living room as usual, and during the night I relived an incident that occurred when I was much the same age as my granddaughter. My father is rubbing his penis all over my two-year-old tummy. He ejaculates and rubs the semen in. As he does, he also stimulates me to orgasm. I experienced this both visually and physically in a half-awake state. When later I awoke fully, I felt stunned and shocked and disoriented. I didn't talk about it with anyone but the memory didn't fade. It was very vivid and deeply disturbing. I was no longer able to change my granddaughter's nappies as I felt I would contaminate her unsullied spirit and trust in me if I did. So, I just made an acceptable excuse whenever the need arose.

Some years later, when I started to reconnect with my sister, I asked her about the time Mum was so ill and we slept in the living room. She told me that this did indeed happen, and she was obviously surprised that I remembered it, given my young age at the time.

# Crawling to the Letterbox

In 2017 I was examined by Canberra psychiatrist Bruce Lean (now deceased) in order to authorise the prescribing of Xanax by my GP Suzanne Davey. Dr Lean wrote the following report:

*Dear Suzanne*

*RE: Ms Elizabeth Mamchak DOB: 09/01/1944*

*Thank you for referring Elizabeth who attended for consultation 15/08/2017.*

*As is clear from your comprehensive referral and what came to light in my consultation with Liz, is the complexity of her situation.*

*I agree she has Panic Disorder not responsive to other medication and clearly benefited by Alprazolam. I therefore support your continued prescribing of Alprazolam 0.5.mg up to 1 b.d.pm.*

*Co-morbidly, she has complex PTSD and Major Depressive Disorder all relatively controlled at the moment by Efexor XR 150mg @mane and her own endeavours over the years.*

*Liz touched on her health conditions which recently have been quite dramatic but currently in remission – I understand you and her other specialists are managing them. I have stated to Liz that should you or she have any concerns in the future, I am happy to be consulted per 'phone', fax or email and hope I can give helpful advice to keep her hard-won emotional equilibrium in status quo.*

*Kind Regards,*
DR BRUCE LEAN
CONSULTANT PSYCHIATRIST

This report by Dr Bruce Lean was affirming in a way I had not previously experienced other than with my GP Suzanne Davey. Dr Lean stated that I had complex PTSD, a condition I believe I had been striving to understand and manage for most of my adult life. But more than that, he acknowledged in just a few short words that I had contributed to managing this mental health condition by my own endeavours over the years and had been successful in gaining this hard-won emotional equilibrium. I suspect few survivors born in the 1940s and 1950s received this sort of validation and it meant the world to me to be acknowledged in this way. It reminded me of how, when I told my sister, a doctor, how the condition of post-traumatic stress disorder explained so much to me, she responded that it was, 'a useful construct'. I felt gutted. Relegating PTSD to a construct diminished what I was trying to communicate – that it described what I had been suffering from for much of my life.

Before the trauma of war was given formal medical recognition, particularly with the suffering of Vietnam War veterans in the 1970s, awareness of PTSD was limited. This period also saw the rise of the women's movement, advocating for victims of violence, and the acknowledgement of children sexually abused at home. For survivors like myself, struggling with disabling behaviours that seemed inexplicable, it was a long and difficult journey. Claire Weekes, a general practitioner, was a beacon of hope in this dark landscape. Weekes wrote and published a series of books for sufferers of disabling anxiety in the 1960s, 70s and 80s. She understood the effects of anxiety on those who suffered it in a way the psychiatric branch of medicine seemed not to. She wrote with enormous compassion and encouraged her reader-patients at every twist, turn and setback. I believe if she had been born later – she was born in 1903 – she would have made a connection between fear and panic and childhood abuse, both physical and sexual. I discovered Claire Weekes and her approach to healing from nervous suffering, in my never-ending search for a cure. I put into practice her approach to overcoming the panic. It wasn't enough on its own as I needed to also understand the root cause of the fear, terror and panic and the manner in which traumatic memory was stored. But I found her books offered not only encouragement but recognition of how these 'nervous disorders' affected so many aspects of everyday living in a way that no other books on anxiety managed to do. I've read recently of instances where Claire Weekes' teachings and guidance have helped people in this century, although she died in June 1990. She must have been a remarkable person. Understanding the impact my father's sexual abuse had on my mental health didn't happen overnight. It was a process. Some months after I gave up alcohol in January 1984, I went through a period of severe agoraphobia. My house was built on a battleaxe block and the letterbox was at the end of a long drive. My feelings of terror were such that I would imagine myself crawling on hands and knees up the driveway to collect my mail. I felt completely exposed, to what I didn't know, but for some months leaving the safety of my home was cause for a panicked response. I was continually afraid. The anticipation of simple, everyday tasks like driving to the shops, grabbing a trolley, selecting the groceries and waiting in a queue to be served at the checkout was filled with terror.

Along with driving, and venturing outside my safety zone, anything that had the potential of causing me to feel trapped was likely to trigger fear and possible panic. This covered an enormous range of ordinary, everyday situations such as visiting the hairdressers, going to a movie, sitting in a concert, washing my hair in the shower, being held in conversation by someone who talked at me instead of with me, visiting the dentist and being trapped in the dentist's chair, waiting in a queue or sitting on a bus or a train. The 1970s was a time before ATMs and Eftpos and ready access to cash. To withdraw money necessitated a trip to the bank, physically filling in a withdrawal slip and presenting it to the teller along with one's bank book. For reasons I couldn't understand at the time, I wasn't able to sign my name on the withdrawal slip while I was in the bank. My hand shook so violently that my signature was illegible. I overcame this problem by taking a stack of withdrawal slips home and, when needed, filling one in and signing it. The uncontrollable shaking didn't occur when I was away from the public glare of the bank.

I always knew this incapacity was psychological in origin. I believe it was, in part, because I had no sense of who I was. It was almost as though I didn't exist. My father's career in finance, and the way he used money as a form of control, probably played a part in my difficulty proving who I was when completing a financial transaction in a bank. Another memory, sometime later, is of standing in a short queue at the Manuka ATM of the Commonwealth Bank and being overwhelmed by panic. It was the late 1980s and I recognised even then that the panic was connected to the fact that this was the branch of CBA where my father did his banking. I believe that the subconscious mind gathers all the pertinent, stored information when deciding what it should regard as significant. In this case, my conclusion is that it sent out an alarm at the connection between the Manuka branch of CBA, my father and myself.

These days I can sign my name in a public place, although when signing important documents like my will or an application for a passport, my mind darts back for a couple of seconds to the time when I couldn't do it.

Panic, combined with the horrific trans-Tasman experience I had endured many years before, seriously inhibited my ability to travel by air for some twenty-five years. For decades, much of my life was limited by the many and diverse things I was unable to do. I accepted these limitations, as I knew from my own persistent searching that there was no easy quick fix, and I continued to rely on medication to achieve some semblance of a normal life.

I can share a few snapshots that remain strong in my mind from times when I found myself out in the world, having to navigate my way through a panic situation.

\*\*\*

I recall an episode from the 1970s when I was in my car driving towards Kings Avenue bridge, a route I took at least three times a week to attend my job as counsellor at the Educational Program for Unemployed Youth (EPUY). I was running late and felt a surge of anxiety flood my body. Now was not the time to have a panic attack. The anxiety morphed into fear as I thought about crossing the bridge. *Trapped. Nowhere safe.*

 I pulled into a small parking area, just off to the left at the old public service office called West Block. I tried to slow my breathing and wiped my sweaty palms across the top of my trousers. My vision started to blur. There was a car parked nearby and on impulse, I opened my car door, clambered out with shaky legs and went over to it. A middle-aged couple were sitting in earnest conversation. I knocked on the window, and the woman's face appeared as she wound it down. I blurted out, 'would you mind tailing me over the bridge?' It seemed to me a very sensible request under the circumstances. The woman's eyes widened in confusion and then alarm. She hurriedly wound the window back up, started the car and drove off at speed. I was left nonplussed and hurt and my feelings turned to anger. Anger was the very antidote I needed to defuse the power inherent in the panic. Within a few minutes I was able to set off again and drive almost confidently across the bridge.

***

Thunderstorms have been a source of terror for me ever since I can remember. So much so, that as a young child in Canberra, when I learned from somewhere that rubber had special properties that protected people from lightning, I made sure I had my sandshoes nearby as I got into bed at night, especially if storms were forecast. If a storm broke, I would grab one of the sandshoes, pull it under the covers and hold it close to my body, believing in some mysterious way this would give me complete protection. This terror has not lessened over the decades and when I hear of people being struck by lightning, I am simultaneously filled with horror and wonderment on their behalf. On one occasion in the late 1970s, I was having an intense phone conversation with Cecily Parker, a counsellor with whom I had frequent contact, when a storm broke right overhead. I found myself on the floor, curled into a foetal position, continuing our conversation. I could not reveal just how frightened I was as I worked my way through the panic.

\*\*\*

On a clear autumn evening my friend Judy's husband took a group of her friends and me out to dinner, as a thank you for looking after Judy while he was away working on oil rigs. We were taken to the fancy restaurant on the top of Red Hill just above a gelato bar, where we were seated at a long table which afforded a commanding view over Canberra. I didn't know the other guests well and Judy was at the other end of the table. However, I was able to make small talk with those seated either side of me. I was aware that I felt anxious, but I thought it was manageable. My body knew otherwise. When my chosen meal arrived, I discovered I was unable to swallow. I chewed and chewed and pushed the food back and forth around the plate trying desperately to hide my inability to eat. This was my one and only experience of globus hystericus, otherwise known as hysterical lump!

\*\*\*

Huntsmen spiders have always reduced me to a quivering mass. I can look at redback spiders, which are infinitely more venomous, and not react. But huntsmen, which we called tarantulas in Canberra in the 1950s, became a phobia when I was very young. I trace it back to sitting on the floor in a music class at Canberra

Grammer school in Deakin with one of my favourite teachers, whose name I forget but whose buck teeth I remember well. I used to pretend I too had buck teeth by sticking a wad of chewing gum under my top lip and speaking with a lisp. I was about six at the time, it was winter, and we were wearing our dark green tunics under our green blazers with the white school logo on the front. I slowly became aware, as did many of the pupils, of a large huntsman firmly pinned to the left side of the blazer worn by one of the students seated nearby. I froze in horror. My memory goes blank at this point, however I relive that fear every time I encounter a huntsman spider.

\*\*\*

While struggling with the extreme restrictions of anxiety, panic attacks and agoraphobia, in 1984, I heard about a course for individuals suffering from agoraphobia. It was facilitated by two psychologists from the Mental Health Unit of ACT Department of Health. I was interviewed by David, one of the psychologists, who assessed my suitability for the course. During the interview he told me that agoraphobia was not uncommon with incest survivors. This gave me another piece of the abuse puzzle I could slip into place when viewing the whole picture. The location of the course wasn't far from where I lived, so I was confident I would be able to attend after I had worked out the least stressful way of driving there. The meaning of least stressful was the route with the fewest number of stop lights and intersections to be negotiated, both of which were situations likely to cause panic.

I still have the course working sheets and a detailed record of how I managed to move from being confined in the home to being once again part of the community. As participants, we were taught through exposure to the feared situations, while being supported by the facilitators and implementing the coping tools we learned at the beginning of each session. In an article on exposure therapy and coping tactics, AM Jones says 'Our primary aim is to enter and remain in the situations we associate with fear. If it comes, we will face it, and practise whatever coping strategies we have selected.' This statement sums up the fundamentals of the course developed by Tony Jones, a psychologist with ACT Mental Health branch. Implementing the course involved regular relaxation training, listing a hierarchy of places avoided because of past episodes of panic and then venturing into these places with a trained support person to help monitor the fear reaction and encourage the active use of relaxation techniques to lower the intensity of the fear.

How simple it sounds and how challenging it was! It required commitment and a belief in the process on the part of the participants, and compassion, skill and ability to encourage participants through setbacks and feelings of failure on the part of the facilitators. It was a life changer for me.

# Stigma

When I gave up alcohol, I had no expectations of instant recovery, and none occurred. As a sober person I started to feel the pain with greater intensity. However, I felt more able to navigate the obstacles that besieged me. I enrolled in a professional writing course at the then Canberra College of Advanced Education and my partner at the time would drive me to lectures. When that wasn't possible, I would listen later to them on tape. I took the course because, tucked deep inside, was the belief that I had a story to tell.

The decades that followed were a strange combination of personal achievement and struggle. I pursued a wide range of therapies, including massage and deep tissue bodywork and counselling with a psychologist. I hoped to achieve a breakthrough in which the persistent panic and subsequent despair would magically disappear, and I would be free to live what I viewed as a 'normal' life. So much energy was expended juggling my mental health problems alongside my work life, never recognising the impact one had on the other. Mental illness was very much stigmatised at this time, and while I supported efforts to remove the stigma, I still fell victim to the shame. I battled with the belief that depression and anxiety, the medical terms used then to describe my condition, were the result of some personal weakness and could be overcome through sheer determination. Had I been able to talk freely about the inner turmoil that was causing me such distress, I might have managed better. I strove instead to hide my perceived failings. I must have talked about them to my father when I was drunk, as I later discovered his notes about phone conversations held with my siblings about my mental health problems. I transcribe some of his notes below:

> *9/2/79 Ish [Elizabeth – me] As Observed: FW [Fred Wheeler] & Flip [Philip] & D [Donelle – Philip's wife]*
> (A) *Subject to extremes of emotion & behaviour ie swinging from frenetic "highs" to frenetic "lows" & the lows being characterised by energetic aggressiveness.*
> (B) *Also noticeable, if it be a separate fact, intermittent bouts of "panic" or bouts of "loss of confidence" "can't cope" manifested in such ways as*
>> (1) *"refusal" or "inability" to drive a car*
>> (2) *lack of attendance at family pre-arranged social w/or family occasions*
>> (3) *fears about, or lack of fulfilment of job arising out of her engagement as a "counsellor" at the Canberra*
>
> **TAFE College**
> *Also noted that whenever she "wants" (wishes) to do (achieve) something she drives ahead in a most forceful & efficient manner very intelligent & efficient Also noted that is very self centred & self loves to be the centre of attention"*

*Pam: Friday 2/5/79: 1.00 pm*

*Lots family contact*

Liz: Contact unsatisfactory
Always will be.
Got people on a string – everybody ?
Has had some "downs"
But basically selfish self indulgence
<u>manipulative</u> histrionics
Drinking to excess.
Maybe an underlying condition
But so much selfish overlay
Been given help but doesn't help
herself.

Intelligent but gets something out
of the manipulative histrionics
Hell-bent on own self-destruction
Upsetting Flip

I was deeply hurt to read these records of conversations my father had with my brother and sister and former sister-in-law. I was drinking to excess but the comments about my behaviour felt judgemental and harsh. They were damning and plain unkind. I wondered if either sibling had ever stopped to question why I suffered from disabling panic and depression.

There was something else in these notes that was peculiar to the Wheeler family dynamics. My father had the ability to get information from people. Between the lines, I recognised his method of interrogation at work. I sensed that my sister and brother had a need to tell him what he wanted to hear, and in return they would win his favour. He had this uncanny ability to get people to give him information about other people without realising just how much they were divulging. I know this because I had been caught up in this game of his on many occasions in my own quest for his approval.

# Shame

One of the more puzzling effects of child sexual abuse is the shame commonly felt by victim-survivors. It defies all reason that an innocent child, who is blameless for the act of sexual exploitation perpetrated by an older, more powerful adult would feel shame. But research and anecdotal reports tell us that they do.

The reasons for this shame are complex. Shame can be transferred from the perpetrator to the victim and survivor shame can also result when the child victim participates in sexual acts to please or placate the perpetrator, especially when the abuser is a parent or a close family member.

Shame is associated with doing something bad, like lying or cheating or stealing or failing to live up to one's expectations of oneself. 'I should have known better.' When an abuser tells the child victim, 'look what you made me do' or states 'you know you've been asking for this', the child feels to blame. Implicit in the abuser's accusation is the judgement 'you made me do this bad thing,' which results in the child taking on the badness of the adult's sexual abuse and feeling ashamed. This strategy of denying all responsibility for the abuse is common among perpetrators.

Another source of shame for the child is if they experience pleasure while being abused. This presents the child with conflicting feelings. The child victim mistakenly believes they must have wanted the abuse if they experience these strangely pleasurable sensations. I understand this shame well as my father would stimulate me to orgasm when I was very little, and, while the intense feeling of physical pleasure was undeniable, I felt confused and deeply ashamed of my body's involuntary response. Over time, sexual arousal became entwined with fear, and fear would then be accompanied by arousal, which was further cause for shame. When shame is internalised and maintained in silence, it will fester and seep into so many areas of the child's being, thus embedding a negative self-image and low self-esteem.

As a society, we've made some progress in acknowledging that child sexual abuse is widespread and found across all walks of life. It is now reported much more widely in the media, as is the making and distribution of child pornography. And yet at an individual level there is still a reluctance to acknowledge it. My personal experience is that when people hear any detail of the abuse, it is resisted as being nasty, disgusting, even. This is understandable. However, the impact on the adult survivors reinforces the feelings of shame. I have on occasion disclosed to persons with whom I am not close, and I have felt a wall come up which said, 'Don't say anymore – I don't want to know.' The result was that I felt ashamed, as though I had done something wrong. Participants on a forum for adult survivors that I follow express feelings of shame again and again. The accepted answer, 'but you weren't to blame' is totally inadequate. It fails to look at why the shame developed in the first place.

In July 2022 I tuned into ABC radio to listen to *Conversations*. In this episode, Sarah Kanowski interviewed author and political analyst Sisonke Msimang. Learning about Sisonke's background and upbringing was fascinating, but it was her description of an incident she experienced as a young child in Canada that gave me pause for thought. Sisonke and her sister were the only black children in her school. On one occasion, Sisonke was playing on the monkey bars in the playground when another student pointed at her and said, 'look at the monkey on the monkey bars.' Sisonke was devastated. She ran home to her parents in tears and told them about the racist taunt. Her father, a freedom fighter and man of great physical stature, insisted on going back to the school with Sisonke, despite her intense embarrassment, to speak to the principal and to demand an acknowledgement of the racism and an apology. Sisonke's teacher explained to the class how this racist affront had hurt Sisonke and asked that the whole class apologise, which they did. Sisonke completed her story by saying that she felt no shame as a result of this racist name-calling because the offence was acknowledged, and an apology was given.

For me this was a telling moment. Ah-ha! I thought... this is what's needed to dispel those feelings of shame that are carried so often by survivors of child sexual abuse. And this is what victim-survivors rarely, if ever, receive from their abusers. Recognising what was needed to resolve those feelings of shame, while accepting that it will never happen, allowed me to explore other ways of lessening the anguish. The most satisfactory answer appears to be to change societal attitudes and responses rather than targeting individual responses. This suggestion is not new. But it could make a real difference. Grace Tame is a strong advocate of this approach.

The origins of shame are complex and the precise elements vary for each individual. Perpetrators often use the threat of dire consequences if the victim were to reveal the abuse. 'I (the abuser) would be sent to prison' or 'you would have to go into care'. The perpetrator needs to maintain silence in order to keep on abusing. These threats are worded in such a way that the child victim is drawn into the abuse and feels at least partially to blame for what is being done to them. And because it must be kept secret it must also be 'bad' and therefore a reason for feeling ashamed.

As Oprah Winfrey, American journalist, TV talk-show host, sexual abuse and rape survivor summed it up well in a 2019 interview with *People* magazine. 'And if the abuser, the molester, is any good, they will make you feel that you are complicit, that you were part of it. That keeps you from telling.' It also magnifies the victim's feelings of shame.

Society reinforces victims' shame by discouraging open and honest discussion of sexual assault in general and child sexual abuse in particular. The secrecy and silence surrounding child sexual abuse and, to an even greater extent, incest, create feelings of shame for the child victim. Secrecy and silence are the perpetrators' weapons of choice. Dismantling the wall of silence brick by brick, carefully and deliberately, using the voices of survivors, will go a long way in lessening the shame carried by victim-survivors.

# Manipulation and Control

I was working as a community social worker when I counselled a male client who had difficulty hearing. I asked him how his hearing loss came about, and he told me that, when he was growing up, his father would bash his head against the fridge as punishment. This happened not once but again and again. And there was the woman who, recounting the domestic violence she endured, showed me how she lost all her front teeth from being punched mercilessly in the face by her partner. This type of violence sounds shocking and is shocking.

I don't remember my father being physically violent, other than to thrash my sister and me with the clothes brush as punishment, during our early years growing up in Canberra. The word thrash, the very word used by my parents, has a ring of violence to it. While I don't have any visual memory of being thrashed, my body remembers it as a stinging sensation on my buttocks. I can still see the shape and colour of the clothes brush and where it would rest on my father's low-boy.

My father inflicted a much quieter and more insidious kind of violence when he abused me. For child sexual abuse, whether loud and angry or quiet and insistent and cajoling, is violence. Playing on my desperate need for his recognition and approval, he could manipulate me into compliance. But he was neither tolerant nor understanding in day-by-day living, especially when he felt put upon.

Once I returned home to Canberra for the university holidays after a break-up with my boyfriend. I was shattered as only teenagers can be, and spent endless hours in my room, playing mournful operatic arias over and over. The music reflected my despair and allowed me to indulge my anguish. I vividly recall how, just as my mother was about to drive me back to Women's College for the next academic term, my father farewelled me by saying, 'and next time, don't bring a black cloud with you.' This was delivered flatly and coldly. As we drove down the street, heading for the road out of Canberra, I asked my mother in bewilderment, 'Why does he hate me so much?'

My father ruled with words and tone of voice. He must have taught me to be afraid of him at an early age, as my fear response was deeply ingrained. On a visit to Canberra from New Zealand with my then husband and my eldest daughter, I remember an incident when my father elicited such a fear response in me that I lost control of my bladder and wet myself. I was in my early twenties, a married woman and mother. I have no memory of what led to this painful humiliation, nor do I remember what happened afterwards. And yet I clearly remember the red and white striped pants suit I was wearing.

When my husband and I decided to separate in Lafayette, Sandy later told me that he spent three quarters of an hour on the phone with my father, answering all manner of questions about the separation and the decision that I would return to Canberra to live. He described the conversation as an interrogation rather than a concerned discussion about my welfare or the children's.

When I returned to Canberra, the children and I stayed with my parents initially. The children slept in one bedroom, and I slept on the fold-out Parker bed in another bedroom. One night my father came into my bedroom and put his hands under the bedclothes, to fondle my breasts. I feel a surge of anger as I recognise, all these years later, how he preyed on my emotional vulnerability. A few short months later, he did it again when Sandy and I went on holiday to Fiji as a way of reconciling. By then, the children and I had moved into a flat in Red Hill. My father invited me out to dinner with him at The Lobby restaurant, while my mother babysat. I have no idea how long we were at the restaurant before my father reduced me to tears, by stating flatly, 'unless you tell me what went wrong sexually with your marriage, your mother won't look after the children when you meet up with your husband.' While I was still in tears, my father took me back to his place in Red Hill, had me sit on his knee under the guise of comforting me, and started fondling my breasts. He said 'I admire you for being so broadminded about incest.' Even now, I feel the most overwhelming shame, as I recall how my body responded to his touch. This feeling vies with the most furious rage, as I yell in my head, 'How dare you? How dare you hit on your daughter when she was at her most vulnerable and fuck her up still further?' I wish I could have shouted these words back then, but I didn't have the courage or the confidence. What better way to ensure that the reconciliation would ultimately fail? My father knew exactly what he was doing.

To knowingly manipulate me, his daughter, to feel shame, confusion, unwanted sexual arousal and resultant self-loathing... these actions are close to being evil.

# Not Being Believed

If asked why they didn't tell someone about the abuse long ago, survivors usually reply, 'I didn't think anyone would believe me.' This is understandable. The closer the relationship of the victim to the perpetrator, the less likely they will be believed, even though research by the Australian Bureau of Statistics (2019) tells us 'the majority of persons who experienced child sexual abuse knew the perpetrator and experienced multiple incidents of abuse'. Family members, especially parents, are not readily accepted as perpetrators. They are literally too close to home.

Abuse by a member of the clergy or molestation by a sports coach or a scout master is somewhat distanced and therefore more likely to be believed. Survivors of clergy abuse and other institutional abuse have told their stories to the Royal Commission into Institutional Sexual Abuse and their stories have been documented in the Commission's report. These stories hit you in the gut. But there has been no such public enquiry into child sexual abuse perpetrated by family members since the 1976 Royal Commission into Human Relationships, even though this constitutes a large percentage of all child abuse. Michael Salter, an expert on violence against women and child sexual abuse, argues strongly for the need for such an enquiry, while looking into the reasons it has been avoided for so long, in his paper, 'The privatisation of incest: The neglect of familial sexual abuse in Australian public inquiries'. Salter explores how and why incest manages to avoid public scrutiny by hiding in the shadows of the privacy of the family, stating, 'the efforts of the women's movement to articulate the political significance of incest in the 1970s and 1980s have been wound back by a persistently individualising and pathologising logic that construes incest cases as a series of private aberrations rather than a public problem.'

I know how it feels when you are not believed. It is more than a rebuff. Denying such a fundamental part of my life experience is also a denial of how those experiences fed into the person I became. I didn't ask to be abused but I live with the impact on my life and how it has shaped who I am in so many fundamental ways. The abuse has affected my belief in myself, my capability, my relationships and my parenting. I have experienced cycles of deep depression and lived in a state of terror for periods of time that seemed endless. Panic has dramatically constricted my capacity to travel freely and to socialise easily. And for many years varying degrees of agoraphobia severely curtailed my ability to perform daily activities like shopping and caring for my children. I still need to plan outings carefully, always allowing plenty of time, and I find spur-of-the-moment decisions very stressful. Like most people with a disability, I have learnt to accommodate what I can't do in my life although at times I feel great envy as I see friends driving great distances with apparent ease. More than anything, I feel sadness as I reflect on the years when I didn't understand what was wrong with me – or why – or the many losses that ensued. I believed I was wholly responsible for all that went so wrong in my life, that I didn't try hard enough.

After finding the courage to disclose, it feels like a slap in the face to not be believed. In whatever way the 'not believing' is expressed, it's akin to saying, 'you're lying'. Being called a liar is crushing and destructive. It is an accusation that goes to the very essence of a person's being. It's a damning judgement. I've been accused of fabricating, which is just a fancy way of saying you are making this up, which in turn is a softer way of saying 'you're lying'. None of the softening of language lessens the impact of the message.

A BBC program I heard in the wee hours one morning in 2014 gave me a better understanding of why people deny the child sexual abuse perpetrated by someone close to them.

Put simply, if someone you know well is accused of sexually abusing a child, you need to re-evaluate that person with the allegations of sexual abuse in mind. If the alleged perpetrator was held in high esteem and much admired in the community, those close to them might question both their world view and their judgement. At the very least, the questions raised are disturbing. Some friends from my childhood have chosen to not believe me, and I wonder if it is because they need to hold onto their long-held view of my father. I can appreciate this need to maintain a safe and secure view of the world and those who inhabit it. However, I feel deeply hurt at not being believed. I feel diminished. Denial is about protecting the emotional ease and comfort of the denier as it repudiates what is alleged by the victim-survivor.

According to the Royal Commission on Institutional Sexual Abuse, it takes an average of twenty-three years and nine months for a survivor to disclose the abuse. Those years can be tumultuous for survivors who, while working on fallout from the abuse, continue to examine and re-examine their memories. I have yet to meet an abuse survivor who does not carefully examine the truth of what they remember. Child sexual abuse is not normal, so it is not surprising that victim-survivors question the truth of this depraved behaviour. Indeed, making sense of it, especially when it is perpetrated by a close relative, who is in a position of authority, whose responsibility it is to care for and protect the child, can distort the child's sense of self and trust in the world.

My father's career and standing in government circles in Canberra posed yet another obstacle for me to overcome in disclosing his abuse and I believe it afforded him extra protection. He was employed in Department of Treasury before we left for Geneva. After holding the position of Treasurer to The International Labour Organisation for eight years he returned to Canberra at the end of 1960 to take up the position of Chairman of the Commonwealth Public Service Board. He was knighted in 1967 and appointed as Secretary to the Treasury in November 1971. These positions were high profile in public service circles and, in particular, in Canberra in the 1960s, 1970s and 1980s. Canberra was still a small town then, full of gossip and a degree of backbiting, according to my mother. My father's name, Wheeler, was well known. The positions he held were powerful. I absorbed the feeling of power my father wielded and was intimidated by it.

Child sexual abuse and incest were denied at this time or regarded as a problem of the uneducated and the poor. It was much easier to reposition such an uncomfortable truth rather than face up to it. I was very aware of my father's standing in the community. I remember attending a fund-raising activity for the soon to be Prime Minister Gough Whitlam in the early 1970s and, when introduced to Whitlam as Wheeler's daughter, Whitlam commented, 'I didn't expect to see a daughter of Wheeler's here.'

I wasn't privy to the gossip in Canberra, but it must have still been rife in the 1990s and would explain why, at my father's wake, I was pursued by a drunken stranger who persisted in asking me if I had reconciled with my father.

I accompanied my father to Government House when he received the Companion of the Order of Australia in 1979. I don't remember much about the presentation. but I do remember being impressed by the stunning design of the medal. I always felt conflicted about the awards my father received. I could appreciate his achievements in career terms but as I came to better understand how my mental health problems were the result of the incest, I found it hard to reconcile his career achievements with my abuse. Dr Maxine Tennant, whom I saw following the mugging and who asked if I had been abused, commented that I must be proud of my father's achievements. I recoiled physically when she said this and was taken aback that even she was caught up in the Canberra adulation of status.

# The Hidden Side of Abuse

Abuse is always ugly. But for me, the really nasty side of the abuse lay in the degrading and demeaning behaviour I exhibited on occasion. And it was not always fuelled by alcohol. It was behaviour over which I had no control, and which followed a pattern learnt from childhood.

As a fifteen-year-old in Geneva, looking at least eighteen, I would hang out in cafes drinking coffee and smoking cigarettes. I imagine I portrayed a certain sophistication and the one thing I had confidence in was my ability to attract men. On reflection, it was the only attribute I had confidence in, and I used it to exercise a power that I didn't feel in any other area of my life. I would go to cafes in the old town of Geneva or to a cafe down by the lake, drinking coffee and smoking cigarettes, always alone, picking up much older men. I knew how to give glances and looks that invited contact. I didn't have sex with these men as pregnancy was a constant fear, but I did put myself at risk. I was lucky I didn't get raped, bashed or worse. Strangely, I have no feelings of shame as I remember this early promiscuous behaviour. It's when I started to drink excessively and sleep indiscriminately with men in the years after I lost my older two children that I feel the deepest, most scarifying shame. I am appalled. I put my younger daughter at risk in many ways and this is a source of enormous guilt, sadness and regret. She commented to me once that she was lucky she wasn't molested as a child. How could I respond to such an honest and perceptive comment, other than to agree?

I have always believed that alcohol only frees up destructive and shameful behaviour; it doesn't cause it. My indiscriminate sleeping around and one-night stands during my thirties, would be called 'acting out' by psychologists. This makes sense to me. It was all about taking charge and being in control. These encounters weren't a source of sexual pleasure but a means of reversing the power imbalance. I dictated the terms.

The most dangerous incident followed an admission to the psychiatric unit at Calvary hospital. A male patient developed an obsession with me and took my details from my hospital wristband. He turned up at my house after I was discharged, and I acquiesced to him moving in. I was there alone at the time. This man was severely alcoholic and full of promises of all the things he would do to help me maintain my home. Like so many alcoholics, he was all talk and no action. I resumed my heavy drinking following discharge from hospital and sank once again into the twilight zone where everything was a muted grey with no sharp outlines. It wasn't long after his arrival that this man, whom I later learned was wanted by the police in New Zealand, turned on me and started lashing out verbally. I have no memory of what triggered this sudden change in attitude. I probably asked him to leave. He told me he would 'cut my face to shreds.' I believed him as he had told me of his previous criminal behaviour. I told him I needed to Dial a Prayer and, very quietly, rang the police. It took two carloads of police to remove him from my house as I watched, terrified. I remained full of fear until I learnt from persistent contact with the police, that he had been deported to New Zealand to face criminal charges.

I was admitted to hospital several times for drinking and overdosing on prescription medication. The admission I remember most clearly was that following my drunken response to the death of my close friend and boss Ray, who died from leukaemia. I was in the Calvary psychiatric unit for about three weeks. There was very little offered in the way of treatment and a fellow patient and I joined together in stirring up trouble. I must have given social worker as my occupation because I remember the slightly bemused welfare officer, who was attached to the ward, laying down the law about specific rules to be observed, which we promptly broke.

During this hospital stay my father would drive to the hospital every lunchtime and sit with me until his lunch hour was over, when he would drive back to the office. He didn't ask how I was or what had led to me being admitted. I don't remember any conversation although we must have exchanged pleasantries. He always had some paperwork and I would sit obediently not uttering a word. The senior social worker from Woden Hospital, where I had been employed, visited me and commented on how fortunate I was to have my father visit every day. I didn't reply in any sensible way as I couldn't understand why he turned up day after day, to work on some unknown task and then left. It has always seemed to me that he was giving me a silent message about keeping quiet.

From time to time a cruel and destructive part of me has taken over. I have only regret at the hurt I have caused others during these unprovoked verbal assaults. I have examined these incidents carefully, trying to understand what caused them and why I reacted so strongly. It might have been a comment that touched a nerve so deep and hidden that anger out of all proportion would rise up and propel me into a verbal response so ferocious and vicious that even I would be taken by surprise. I lost a couple of important friendships as a result. I remember one instance when my younger daughter said something that could have been uttered by my father. It was as if I was being dismissed as of no value, and I reacted by digging my fingers into her arm and intentionally hurting her.

As a child, my response would always be physical because I didn't have the words to express the rage, let alone understand what caused it. When I was in my early teens and my family were staying at the mountain resort with Australian family friends for a skiing holiday, the middle daughter in the family commented at breakfast one morning that my father was very mean with money. This comment, which certainly had some truth in it, provoked such anger in me that I physically beat the girl up. My father ordered me to apologise to the girl's parents as well as to the girl herself. I felt something about the whole incident was not right, but I had no means of adjusting the balance as I didn't fully understand the dynamics at play.

This need to protect the abusive parent is well recognised and documented. The child cannot afford to bring the abuse into the light as doing so will put her relationship with the abusive parent at risk. So, a continual juggling of 'knowing the truth' versus 'maintaining the silence' operates. To make this easier, the child internalises the feelings of badness and shame that belong to the perpetrator, in the belief she or he deserves the abuse. This lays the foundation for deep-seated feelings of worthlessness, which can persist for a lifetime.

# Reflections on My Mother

My mother was a striking looking woman. She was slender with green-hazel eyes and an aloof manner, probably a combination of shyness and vanity. The vanity is speculation on my part, but she wouldn't wear glasses and a certain loftiness was the result. She had very good dress sense and looked stunning in evening gowns. I think appearance was important to her, a means of bolstering her self-confidence.

But who she was beyond this surface exterior, I honestly don't know. There are so many things I never asked her, such as the story of her early life and what her hopes and dreams were. My father always held her up as the epitome of motherhood and he implied that she had sacrificed everything for her children. I accepted this without question for much of my life, just as I accepted almost everything I was told. We children were not allowed to question my father's idealised view of my mother. He recorded the words 'vilification of Peg' in his notes about me at a time when he deemed that I had spoken unfavourably about my mother. As I examined my family of origin in greater detail, I had to acknowledge that this depiction of my mother didn't ring true. My mother has always been a shadowy figure to me. When I try to describe her as a person, it's usually in terms of the roles she fulfilled, not who she was as an independent person. In Switzerland she developed a passion for visiting European countries, but as I rarely accompanied her on these travels, I didn't witness or share in her excitement and exploration of new places.

She must have inherited the British tradition of valuing a son and heir from her own mother, who was English by birth. From the little I know of my mother's upbringing she wasn't much prized as a daughter by her mother, who lost a son in infancy. This may account for my mother's obvious favouritism of my brother with whom she shared a strong bond. Perhaps she was able to relax and enjoy him in a way she couldn't with my sister and me. Whatever the reason, she seemed much lighter around my brother, and he was definitely the golden child.

In the early weeks after my two eldest children were born in Rotorua in 1965 and 1968, my mother came to help me. The 1965 visit after my daughter's birth is by far the warmest memory I have of her. I can still see her in her green slacks and matching jumper. It's the most authentic and relaxed memory I have of her. I was a first-time mother, just twenty-one years old, living in a new country, and I was totally ill prepared for motherhood. In addition, I had a newborn baby who was fat intolerant and cried up to eight hours a day. It was nerve-racking, and I was floundering. I felt completely useless. I really needed my mother and for the first time in my memory she was there for me. Every evening Mum and I would sit in the little living room of our rented house in Uta Street rocking my daughter in the pram to soothe her, while poring over Dr Benjamin Spock's well-thumbed copy of *Baby and Child Care*, especially the chapter on newborn babies and crying, searching for answers. There was no pretence and no hiding behind a facade of expertise. Without fanfare, my mother took over all the washing and cooking while I tried to look after this distressed baby. It took another three or so months, in consultation with my doctor, to work out the cause for the incessant crying. However, my mother gave me unquestioning support during my first few weeks at home. I valued this enormously, although nothing quite stopped my heart from sinking when I received congratulatory wishes from friends in Australia. I almost wept as I read the upbeat messages and good wishes and sentiments that spoke of an experience I had not yet had.

Fast forward six years, and I returned to Canberra from Lafayette with my two little children, inwardly distraught and in shock because my marriage had broken down. After the short reconciliation, journeys around country NSW for employment and then a final, permanent separation, I returned, yet again, to Canberra with my children. I had a deeply mistaken belief that returning to Canberra and my parents would solve all my problems. The reality was that my mother was unable to cope with my distress even as I clung to the childlike belief that she could make it all better. I expected her to somehow rescue me, pick up the pieces and put them all back together again. Isn't that what mothers do? But she couldn't do this, still less could she discuss what was happening for me. She reacted with extreme tension of her own, which manifested in the tight set of her lips and a body like a tightly wound coil that looked as though it might burst apart at any moment.

Once, my mother came to my house in Curtin offering to look after my children while I shopped for groceries. I can still see her, sitting on the edge of the sofa, hands clasped together on her lap, so ramrod straight, tense and forbidding. I had a massive panic attack on the way to the shops and turned around and headed home, tearful and defeated, without any groceries.

During these turbulent years I visited my mother fairly often, but these visits were never satisfying. I would leave feeling emotionally empty. I cannot remember any discussion with her after my falling apart which resulted in Sandy taking our children to live with him. At this devastating time, we agreed that I was to recover from my stress breakdown and the children would return to live with me. Sometime later, when I learnt that he had taken my children to New Zealand, I went to my parents' place, completely distraught, seeking comfort and advice. It was my father who laid out my options as he saw them. He posited that I could, a) go to New Zealand and resume the marriage and live as man and wife; b) go to New Zealand and resume the marriage and then bring my children back to Australia; or c) I could accept the situation as it was. The first two options were laughable. I couldn't drive my children to and from school in Deakin, let alone fly to New Zealand and embark on living a lie. And I knew at some level that I couldn't subject my children to any such emotional tug-o-war. I don't remember my mother offering any opinion about the situation. Afterwards we would pretend that it was somehow meant to be. I have no idea what she thought or what she told her friends at her weekly bridge meetings, the litmus test of her public persona.

It's likely that it was she who arranged for the Reverend Jack Tyrrell to come and give me support and comfort. She said on numerous occasions, 'You're so lucky to have Mr Tyrrell.' I was baffled. I didn't feel at all lucky. The Rev Tyrrell had officiated at my wedding to Sandy. My memory is that he started visiting me at home after the children left for New Zealand with their father. I didn't know how to say 'Please don't come', and Mr Tyrrell turned up week after week. I have no memory of discussing anything of significance. I do remember him drinking my sherry and initiating a routine of kissing and fondling me. Like most predators, he knew to zero in on obvious vulnerability. I loathed his sexual advances and can still remember the feel of his dry, scaly lips. When he suggested we go and lie down, which was a euphemism for having sex, it was the very feeling of physical repugnance that gave me the courage to refuse. He didn't return after that. I don't think I processed this episode other than to think how distasteful it was. I now recognise the grooming – however clumsy – of a vulnerable person, followed by the most blatant predatory behaviour. Typical of predators, he was older, an authority figure – chaplain at Canberra Boys Grammar – who behaved as though he had every right to initiate sexual kissing and fondling, followed by a clear proposition of having sex.

When I met Tony, the man who became my second husband and fell pregnant with Emma, my mother was noticeably distant about my pregnancy which I couldn't understand, other than to think it was because I wasn't married. More to the point perhaps, she had witnessed my previous failure to care for my older two children. After her death, I came across a lovely hand-sewn dress she'd had made for Emma, and a bundle of cream and brown squares she had knitted for a rug. These gestures were full of feelings I never saw expressed. She died when Emma was nine months old.

The final chapter of my mother's life was sudden and unexpected and swift. She rang me to tell me she had pain in her hip, and soon after she was admitted to Royal Canberra Hospital. During her first week in hospital, I was struck by how she seemed to blossom. She looked positively radiant. She started to deteriorate in the second week and by the third week she was losing her hair and bruises appeared on her arms. A friend of my mother's gave her a vibrant, purple shawl which my mother kept wrapped around her upper body. I knew, when the sides of the bed came up, that she was dying. My father never acknowledged it, but sat with her day after day, attending to the work matters he brought with him in his briefcase.

In her final week, my mother did have an angry outburst in which she expressed what felt like real resentment towards me. She asked me to take her nighties home so I could wash and iron them, and then return them to her in hospital. I must have hesitated, as I found the almost daily journey really difficult because of the panic. She picked up on this hesitation and hissed at me, 'Well, I washed and ironed all those Grammar uniforms for you, day after day.' This exchange had a huge effect on me. I was deeply upset and have never understood what was at the bottom of her anger. Was it directed at me, her daughter, for some unspoken grievance? Was it because she was dying and no-one around her acknowledged this? Or was it because of unexpressed regrets in her life? I will never know. She was only sixty-one and I believe there was much that was unresolved in her life. In part, this reflected the times. Perhaps it was also influenced by my father's frequent demand, 'don't spill your guts.'

The final act of my mother's life was as sad and empty as those evenings spent talking about what might have been in her own life and what a happy childhood I had. The funeral was private…

for family only. My sister was held up in Hawaii and couldn't be there in time. I later learnt that my father could have delayed the funeral, but chose not to. My sister didn't get to say goodbye. I was there with my brother, his former wife and my father. There was no service, just a coffin with a spray of beautiful flowers on it which, after a certain time, at a signal from my father, disappeared. No words said in memory of my mother. No recognition. No acknowledgement. The final blow came when I visited the crematorium on the first anniversary of her death, with a single rose I wanted to place on my mother's plaque, only to find there was no plaque… Nothing. Nothing to commemorate the life of Peggy Hilda Wheeler.

# Reflections on My Father

2020 brought a year of great change in the form of a pandemic that spread across the globe and with it, serious contemplation of what matters at both an individual and a societal level. The word unprecedented was used so often in the media that it lost much of its impact. The summer of catastrophic bushfires in NSW was followed by a gradual dawning that the virus was real and contagious and lethal. Along with so many others, I spent weeks at home, avoiding contact with anyone who might be carrying the virus. Older people like me were deemed at risk and, because I didn't want to die in hospital, isolated from my children and surrounded by health care workers in gowns and face masks and face shields, I kept strictly to the guidelines and stayed abreast of the daily coronavirus press conferences.

It would have been an ideal time to concentrate on my memoir, but that didn't happen. My reaction to the endless reports of the virus, both nationally and globally, was a restlessness born of powerlessness. Instead of writing, I spent time in my garden where I found a wondrous, all-encompassing sense of calm and beauty.

In the second half of 2020, as Australia started to lift restrictions imposed by the virus, the Black Lives Matter movement took hold in America and rippled across the globe. I could not ignore it and felt deeply troubled by what I heard and read. This movement, as angry and wounded as it was, reverberated in me at different levels. It re-awoke the sense of injustice I felt both personally and for all those survivors who had been abused and were neither heard nor believed. And so, as I worked in my garden, I cast my thoughts to my story and to giving voice to my abuse and to the principal perpetrator of that abuse, my father.

When I think of my father, I still feel a sliver of fear, even now, thirty years after his death. However, if I stand back and observe him in a more dispassionate manner, I see a man who needed to control everything around him. When he couldn't, he would manoeuvre the situation in such a way that he appeared, once again, to be in charge. He did this with an unyielding tone of voice and a slow, deliberate manner of talking. As he spoke, he would flip his cigarette box over and over, in a rhythmical way, which added emphasis to whatever he was saying. When he ordered me – and my daughter and my husband – from his home after I confronted him directly, it was as though banishing me from his presence was the only way he knew to refute my challenge, thereby assuming control once more.

He projected an air of authority and absolute confidence. One of my strongest memories is of him sitting in the living room of his Canberra home at a social or family gathering, with his packet of Dunhill cigarettes and his glass of Corio whisky. From there, he would adeptly direct the conversation. Heated arguments developed on occasion, and he would unobtrusively egg them on. I always got the impression that it was these disagreements that my father most enjoyed. To him it was a game. I never saw him engage in any debate in a way that would expose a vulnerability on his part. In fact, I don't think I ever witnessed him being vulnerable.

He acknowledged my compassion when he wanted me to do something for him. 'Ish, you are much more patient with Joy than I am. She has been on the phone again. Would you go and see her?' Joy had worked with my father at some early stage in his career and she idolised him. However, she also had mental health problems which made a visit for afternoon tea somewhat wearisome, despite her kind-heartedness. My father would cleverly delegate the one-on-one contact with Joy to me, thus avoiding the tedium of a visit himself, while still meeting Joy's need to have contact with a member of the Wheeler family.

Another firmly etched memory is of a small but telling incident that occurred when I lived in New Zealand, and we made a visit across the Tasman to see my parents. Kate, my two-year-old daughter, was wandering around my parents' house holding her dinner on a plate in front of her. Quite by accident, she tipped the plate, so her dinner slid onto the light-coloured carpet in the front hall of my parents' home. My father witnessed the incident and ordered Kate to clean up the mess. She blithely ignored his command and continued to wander. I could sense the fury emanating from him. He found a cloth and forced it into Kate's hand and then directed her hand to the spill on the carpet, attempting to make her clean it up herself. He couldn't accept that this innocent two-year-old child refused to obey him.

I wasn't the only one who felt fear in his presence. I remember clearly at my sister's seventieth surprise birthday in the Hunter Valley chatting to Alf Calvert, a long-time family friend, whom I hadn't seen in decades. Alf, a doctor, and someone I had always regarded as both compassionate and a man of integrity, said to me with a slightly apologetic laugh, 'Actually, I was always a bit scared of your father.' We'd been reminiscing about the past in Canberra, where I had spent my first eight years. I found myself agreeing with Alf and then blurting out that my father had abused me. Alf nodded thoughtfully and replied, 'Ah-ha… that explains a lot of things,' at which moment we were called in to dinner. I didn't have the opportunity to explore any further just what was meant by this remark and Alf has since died.

The story of the promised sixpences illuminates something of my father's character. It is a childhood memory that has never gone away, probably because it was never resolved. It represented my first conscious encounter with betrayal and injustice; the first time I knew something that was clearly wrong. As a child I was taught what was right and what was wrong. I was expected to know the difference and to act accordingly.

When I was seven and in second form at the Church of England Girls Grammar School in Canberra, my marks dropped markedly on one of my term report cards. My teacher commented in my report that I seemed to tire easily and would benefit from the coming holiday. My father's response to this poor performance was to propose that if I improved over the following term, he would give me a sixpence for every A I achieved. I took this very seriously and made great efforts to do well. My report card at the end of the following term had almost all As. I daydreamed about the sixpences I would receive and what I would do with the money. My father never paid up. I couldn't believe he would break a promise so blatantly. I felt completely let down. I also felt, even though I didn't have the words then to articulate it, that I wasn't worthy of his honouring the promise he had made.

The betrayal burrowed under my skin and remained there. Decades later, in my adult years, I reminded him on one occasion of how he still owed me the sixpences plus interest. He responded with dismissive laughter. As I had learnt over the years, this was his way of reducing what I said to being of no importance. Nothing more than a joke.

***

My father, when young, was a man of medium height and a slight build, according to old photos. Over the years he developed a very large paunch, to which excess alcohol and no exercise no doubt contributed. He had a shock of dark hair in his youth which had turned completely white at the time of his death at the age of eighty. He wore a white shirt, maroon tie and maroon socks with his dark suit every day other than on rare holidays. He had multiple shirts, socks and ties, all of the same colour.

My memory of him across the years is that he never hurried and was slow and deliberate in all his movements. This slowness of gait somehow demanded attention from those around him. I don't recall any shared humour with him, and yet he could laugh uproariously when interacting socially. Measured and careful are the traits he personified in almost every facet of his life. He lived by a rigid set of rules, and he had two mantras that he must have used often, given that I remember them so clearly. The first one was 'don't spill your guts' and the second one was 'just give me the facts'. I failed miserably on both counts. And for reasons I never understood, he became very angry if my siblings or I blasphemed, even though he was an avowed atheist.

But for all the rigidity, sex was very important to him and was, I think, bound up in his need for power and dominance. He was an unremitting womaniser, something I witnessed first-hand at the age of nine in our very first house outside Geneva, and later on ski holidays, in the bar, with my mother sitting nearby. And he was a child molester, who sexually abused me at a very young age and as a prepubescent child and continued the abuse well into adulthood.

These different characteristics of my father are consistent with Judith Herman's summation of perpetrators of incest, as she describes them in her book *Father–Daughter Incest*. Herman's review of the research of that time finds that perpetrators have traditional, patriarchal families in which the perpetrator is generally domineering within the family but often well regarded in the community. There are no distinguishing features that set the perpetrators apart. I have not found any research that surpasses this.

As I review memories of long-ago incidents with my father, his behaviour at times strikes me as both deliberately cruel and disturbingly intimate.

When he sidled up to me at a family dinner at his home and whispered so only I could hear, 'As soon as he finds a woman he won't be so loving with the children,' referring to Sandy, after he had taken our children with him to New Zealand. I felt as though I had been punched in the stomach.

Then there were the many times he would call me a self-centred little bitch, starting from when I was ten years old and repeated often, well into adulthood. I didn't understand why I was labelled that way, but when I read his records of conversations with my siblings, during my years of alcohol abuse, he gave the impression that this characterisation had been firmly appropriated by my family of origin.

There was a pathological element to my relationship with my father which I have not been able to completely unravel. It is illustrated in some of his notes about conversations between my father and myself, of which I have no memory but which fill me with shame as I read them. I fail to understand why it took me over half my lifetime to break free from the extraordinary hold he had over me.

Much as I am loath to admit it, seeking my father's approval was the strongest force in my life for decades.

The closest I have come to understanding this destructive force is the chapter on Captivity in Judith Herman's highly regarded book *Trauma and Recovery*. As Herman states, 'Children are rendered captive by their condition of dependency'. And 'In situations of captivity, the perpetrator becomes the most powerful person in the life of the victim, and the psychology of the victim is shaped by the actions and beliefs of the perpetrator'.

My father was the most powerful person in my life, and I measured the men with whom I became romantically involved against him. In a letter to me at Women's College, in November 1963, when I was agonising about my relationship with Sandy, the man I would marry, my brother wrote:

*Dear Liz,*

*You are a mess aren't you? I wonder if you'll ever know your own mind. Anyway, I really don't think you do want someone like Dad – you're too much like him. I know you pretty well and I know that you like to be bossed round to a certain extent but not completely whereas you seem to think you want someone as autocratic as Dad. But I think you have too much strength of character for that & that you would be miserable being told what to do.*

An example of this unhealthy feature of our relationship is when, as a celebration of our joint birthdays in January 1974, my father took my mother, my brother and his former wife, and my new partner and me to The Lobby restaurant for dinner. The only two things I remember about the evening are the long, paisley dress I was wearing and that when I was dancing with my father, I noticed a man on the dance floor with whom I'd had a fleeting sexual encounter. I said to my father, almost conspiratorially, 'there goes a mistake of mine,' to which he responded by laughing with delight. I had learnt over the years how to appeal to his depraved interest in my sex life, even as doing so left me feeling disgusted with myself.

At the funeral and wake of Ray, my boss and mentor from the Psychology Department of Reid TAFE, I drank myself into oblivion and my father was called to pick up the sodden pieces. Through my alcohol-saturated brain, I have a strangely clear memory of two things. The first was of my father arriving with a woman on his arm. I remember that she was wearing black harem pants and high heels. They looked as though they had been out partying. The second thing I remember is that on greeting me, my father said, 'so you're the scarlet woman', distorting the non-sexual relationship I had had with my boss with an insulting throwaway line. Ray, my boss, had believed in me and my work as a psychologist at TAFE. I looked up to him in every way – as a superior, as a mentor and as someone I admired. I'm not convinced my father had any understanding of the complexities and subtleties of relationships. He reduced them to a simplistic black and white, lacking emotional depth, with sex playing a prominent role.

My sense is that it suited him to view relationships in a very traditional, patriarchal way in which the different roles were clearly defined and men were regarded as superior. I didn't witness him seeking women's opinions. I don't think he saw them as of much value. When women did express their views forcefully, he indulged them in a patronising way.

I don't remember him ever asking my opinion about anything, let alone about any aspects of life where I had a deeper understanding than him. He made it clear that he didn't rate the field of psychology highly and he had little regard for counselling. Many years ago, he took my sister and me out to dinner at a restaurant in Narrabundah, called the Nineteenth Hole. Over dinner, my sister Pam and I locked horns about the fact that Medicare only covered physical conditions. I maintained that mental health was every bit as important, and it should be given equal coverage. My sister did not agree at that time, and we argued the topic in a progressively more combative and emotional manner. My father did not offer an opinion either way. He sat back and observed, his mouth twitching in amusement. I could sense his enjoyment in watching this increasingly passionate disagreement evolve.

For him it was pure spectator sport, and he was like a Roman Emperor watching the gladiators of ancient Rome, except the combat was verbal. This incident highlighted what I had so often observed of my father's dispassionate approach to life – it was a game to be played and managed. Succumbing to strong feelings on a topic only weakened a person's position. His approach was black and white and factual which, in my opinion, made him cold and unfeeling. I cannot remember him showing spontaneous empathy at any time. The man I knew was two-dimensional and lacked the very essence that makes us human; the capacity for emotional depth.

# PART FOUR

## Death and Disclosure

# My Father's Death

In August 1994 I received a phone call from my sister telling me that my father was in hospital with a ruptured appendix, and he had asked her to let me know. I was recovering from an accident in which I was struck by a car on a pedestrian crossing and tossed into the air resulting in fractures to the pelvis. I had plenty of free time to sit with this information about my father, and eventually decided to visit him in hospital. By the time he was hospitalised, I had ceased all contact with him, following his complete denial in response to my legal letter. I knew his condition was serious and I needed to see him in case he died. When I made my first visit, I noticed a definite coolness towards me from my siblings. They were civil but not warm. I would learn why in the weeks after the funeral.

My father was in ICU and on a ventilator, so he was unable to speak. I was repulsed by his physical appearance as he lay in the bed, covered by just a sheet. With his enormous stomach, he reminded me of a beached whale. The other memory I have is that visitors spoke over him, as though he wasn't there. It was strange to observe this man who had lived his life always being in control of everything within his reach being stripped of this power, along with his voice. One of the nurses caring for him remarked to me that she thought he was a man used to getting his own way.

My father remained in ICU for three weeks. I visited regularly, and I'm not sure why. I've puzzled about it and haven't come up with a satisfactory answer. I wasn't there out of love, and I certainly had no regrets I needed to express. I thought I saw deep fear in my father's eyes at one stage and I remember thinking, '*no-one should feel that fear.*' I had felt it so often and for so many years. Although I never pinpointed why I visited so frequently, I don't regret that I did.

In the later stages of his hospitalisation, I was the only relative available, as my siblings had returned to their homes in Sydney for a few days. The treating doctor consulted with me about increasing the morphine, pointing out that an increased dose was likely to hasten death. I do remember feeling the enormity of this request as my mind darted from one thought to another to another. I had so often wished for this man's death as I transitioned from the childlike belief in his all-powerfulness to gradually understanding how his sexual abuse of me had so significantly affected almost every facet of my adult life. And yet I felt, momentarily, like a murderess when I told the doctor to proceed.

When it became apparent that my father was nearing the end of his life, and my siblings had returned to Canberra, my sister gave each of us fifteen minutes private time with him. I presume it was to say goodbye and anything else one wanted. I wasn't prepared and reverted to child mode and found myself talking about being OK... Emma and I were just fine. The tone of what I said was almost soothing. All these years later I still don't think accusations or confrontation would have achieved anything, but I do regret that I didn't say how proud I was of myself and my strength in surviving.

As his death drew ever closer, my father was moved into a single room off the main ward. This was to give the family greater privacy.

I contacted my children, and my son Andrew came from Sydney. We were all squashed into this small room, standing around the bed in which my father lay. I was pleased to have Andrew there, but I sensed something that felt like a strong resistance on his part, which I put down to being faced with impending death. My siblings were squeezed into the other side of the room, their aloofness still palpable. They later commented on how upset Andrew seemed at his grandfather's demise. How wrong they were.

It was only in recent years that Andrew told me hadn't slept the night before. He'd been alone in Kings Cross, moving from bar to bar feeding money into pub poker machines; an episode unrelated to his grandfather's declining health. Andrew had developed a compulsive gambling habit. He would turn up to his respectable job at Westpac head office by day, and then slide into self-destruct mode in his own time, away from the view of those who knew him. Andrew described the origins of this silent breakdown as stemming back to an episode when he was twelve years old, when he struggled to connect with reality, and would become paralysed with fear, clutching onto physical objects to reassure himself the world was real. I believe it is likely that these experiences of existential despair had their source many years before this.

***

It was in the early hours of the morning of 5 August that I learnt he was dead. I think it was Wilma, his close friend of many years, who rang. She had been a constant figure at his bedside in the weeks following his burst appendix, and although married and nearer my age than his, she held an important, if hazily defined, role in his life for many years.

I didn't feel anything when I was told that he had died. Nor did his death instantly free me from the effects of the incest, as I had hoped it would. It did, however, open the way for me to start piecing together the many fragments of my sexual abuse story.

OBITUARY: Sir Frederick Wheeler (January 9, 1914 — August 5, 1994)

## Formidable public servant from the old school

Sir Frederick Wheeler was once described as a "legendary public servant and a master of guerrilla warfare in the bureaucracy."

He was also one of Canberra's "seven dwarfs" — Allen Brown, H. C. "Nugget" Coombs, John Crawford, Harry Bland, Dick Randall and Roland Wilson — that remarkable group of top public servants who exercised enormous influence on policy formulation through the Menzies-Holt era of the 1950s and 1960s.

But it was in the Khemlani loans affair, which led to the downfall of the Whitlam Labor Government, that Sir Frederick showed just how formidable was his talent for bureaucratic infighting. What shook Sir Frederick, as Secretary of the Treasury, was that for a brief period during 1974-75 Treasury lost control of the raising of loan funds on the international market, a function it had normally shared with the Reserve Bank. For the Government had turned to a small-time Pakistani commodity dealer, Tirath Hassaram Khemlani, who, through Mr Whitlam's Minerals and Energy Minister, R F X "Rex" Connor, was asked to tap newly-rich oil sheiks for funds to put together a $4 billion loan.

While Sir Frederick was fight-

*Excerpt from the obituary in the Canberra Times*

# The Funeral and the Wake

All funerals are confronting. They remind us that we too will die someday, and so we spend time reflecting on what that means. It becomes more complicated if there was extreme ambivalence towards the deceased person or feelings of regret about important things left unsaid or issues unresolved. Whatever the circumstances, it's usually not an occasion for joy, although it may bring an overwhelming sense of freedom and relief.

I don't think I felt anything at first, although I must have experienced terror at some stage as I wrote a message to myself which said, in bold, black Texta, YOUR FATHER IS DEAD. HE CANNOT HURT YOU ANYMORE. I stuck this message to my bookcase, next to my bed, at the suggestion of my counsellor. It remained there for some weeks until I came to believe it was true.

My father's funeral was held at Norwood Park cemetery on 8 August. It was a day of many contradictions that played out both at the funeral and at the wake. His will stated clearly that he wished to be cremated and that only family members should attend. His funeral was in fact, a public occasion attended by many people including the Governor-General. I chose not to be involved in the arrangements and not to join my siblings in speaking about him. Instead, I wrote out what I would have said and read it to my close friend Marie who accompanied me to the funeral. Unfortunately, I didn't keep a copy, but I recall that I listed the many losses I experienced as a result of the abuse.

I remember the day of the funeral being bitterly cold, as is often the case in August in Canberra. Marie drove me to the crematorium and my younger daughter Emma, my son Andrew and his girlfriend Sue followed separately in another car. There was already a very large gathering when we arrived and I couldn't see any vacant seats until my eyes lit on five empty chairs right at the front, looking at the coffin. Perfect! I strode towards them, stating, 'we are family' only to be intercepted by an usher who declared these seats were reserved for the Governor-General and his entourage. The poor man squirmed with embarrassment as I puffed up with righteous indignation. My friend and I had to squeeze into chairs next to my extended family, while my son, his girlfriend and my daughter found places right up the back. I had really wanted them beside me.

I remember little about the service. My brother told the story of the unusual remedy to ensure my father didn't go into withdrawal, now that he wasn't having his mandatory late morning martinis and double dose of Corio whisky as the day wore on. On being admitted to hospital, the medical team asked him if he had recently abstained from drinking, and if so, how his body had reacted. He responded by saying that some time ago there was a day when he didn't have a drink, and he recalled feeling fine. This clearly didn't reassure them, as a bottle of clear liquid hung at his bedside with a tube going directly into his arm. On the side of the bottle was a strip of masking tape with the handwritten word ALCOHOL on it.

I also remember that I choked on a great big sob as we filed out, causing my former sister-in-law's new partner, whom I didn't know, to comment on how upset I was. The sob did come from a deep place, but the feeling was not about my father's death. It was a recognition that the man being farewelled had never been a father to me. He forfeited that role early in my life. Nothing was quite as it appeared and being upstaged by the Governor-General and separated from my children added to the surreal atmosphere.

The wake continued to add to this strangeness. The alcohol flowed and some man, who apparently knew and greatly admired my father, but whom I did not know, pursued me as he became drunker and drunker, continually asking me if I had reconciled with him. There was some competition about whether my father had been one of the legendary seven dwarfs. This was a reference to the seven height-challenged senior public servants who, according to JR Nethercote, 'rose to so much eminence in Australian government in the Second World War and the post-war reconstruction era'.

My children managed the situation magnificently. The highlight for me was when the wife of my father's colleague at the Public Service Board, swept in saying she just wanted to give me a hug for support, and then left. She had known my father abused me and she had wanted to show her belief in me.

My siblings organised a never-ending supply of grog.

The weirdness of the day reached a crescendo when I was showing Marie the filing cabinet in my father's study, the only piece of furniture from my father's house I had wanted to inherit. I was demonstrating how beautifully the drawers slid on whatever mechanism supported them, when she exclaimed, 'Liz, did you know there is a file on you?' I had absolutely no knowledge of this, so we removed it and, cloak and dagger style, took it out to the car for later examination. A day of high emotion and unexpected happenings. It took me time to process it all, including the significance of what I had found in my father's study.

# The File

Had I not discovered the file my father kept about me, I might not have been as confident about telling my story. I would have been frightened of being relegated to the 'he said–she said' class of stories, mainly told by women; accounts that are, even now, all too readily dismissed. The discovery of the file and what it contained, added credibility to my story.

The file came home with me after the wake, and I opened it as soon as I got in the door. It took a long time before I could make sense of it. I could understand that my father had a copy of my letter from Legal Aid but why so many copies? Why did he have personal letters of mine that dated back to the early 1960s, when I was attending university and living in college? And what was the meaning of the other bits of paper, in his handwriting that were dated and time-recorded? There were too many questions and no ready answers.

At first, I felt a mixture of enormous hurt, with flashes of red-hot anger whenever I looked at the file and its contents. The upset continued for years, clouding my ability to decipher the meaning of the various bits of paper held within this unremarkable manila folder. I needed to approach the file with a clear head so that I could explore the meaning of its contents, free of any strong feelings of anger and distress that might colour what I was reading. This objectivity came little by little and increased as I started to write this memoir. The information within the file exposed an inside view of my father's warped thinking about me.

The contents can be divided into categories:
- Multiple copies of the letter from Legal Aid, written on my behalf by Chris Staniforth, confronting my father about the incest; draft copies of my father's reply and the finished copy; three newspaper articles about recovered memories and False Memory Syndrome, one with sentences underlined.
- Personal letters I received from various close friends, occasional family members and boyfriends and from my first husband-to-be, all of which date back to the 1960s when I lived in Women's College; an invitation to a function in 1962 with the names of former boyfriends written in my father's hand down the side.
- Notes in my father's handwriting of conversations he had about me with family members and their former partners; these conversations took place on the phone in the late 1970s and early 1980s and are all dated and time-recorded by my father. A timeline of my life from birth until mid-1985 in which my father records my birth, countries/places in which I lived, my marriages, the births of my children, my hospital admissions and suicide attempts and my DUI car smash.

On the original letter from Legal Aid with my allegations of 'wrongful acts of incest', my father made the following notations: 'Rec'd 15/7/93: CC: Pam (my sister) Flip (my brother) Nell (my brother's former wife) and two others and 13 copies pls.' Attached to a draft copy of my father's reply to my allegations of incest dated July 1993, was a note from my brother's former wife Nell stating:

'Fred. Some suggested amendments. I do not think counter-allegation (i.e. that this is a devious/vile way to extract money) is helpful. This letter still gives the two messages (1) I deny (2) I will still help & support you. Love Nell.' This note was written on the back of a compliments slip which had 'Rosemary Crowley, Minister Assisting the Prime Minister for the Status of Women' printed on the front. Nell was working for Rosemary Crowley at the time. The suggested amendments to the draft letter are written in ink in Nell's handwriting. On the handwritten letter I wrote to my father stating that I would not be attending his annual Christmas party on 18 December 1993, he has made the following notations: 'My file CC for Pam Flip & Alan Donelle plus 7 in reserve for Kate, Andrew & Emma (my three children) & others if necessary. Initialled (by my father) and dated 16/12/93.'

As I consider the meaning of these annotations on the Legal Aid letter, my father's draft reply and my handwritten letter to my father about the Christmas party – and other documents I have not mentioned – it appears that my father recruited my siblings, their partners and former partners in support of his denial of the abuse. I believe he was drumming up family support in the event of a court case. I see it as a carefully planned, strategic move. I fail to see how else it could be interpreted. Additionally, it explains the coolness I detected from my family of origin when I visited my father in hospital before his death.

I was cast as the dysfunctional, deluded member of the family, and he was building a war chest of artifacts he could use to influence members of my own family, including my children. The confidence of the man can not be doubted!

If the conclusions I reach are indeed correct, my father's power is once again evident. No family member contacted me to ask why I had made these allegations. The support for my father took place without my knowledge. The irony was that I didn't have the emotional strength to even consider pursuing the incest in court because I knew my father would use his calculated and unremitting approach to prove me an unreliable witness. My history of overdoses and alcohol abuse would have given him all the ammunition he needed. He would have destroyed me completely, and without hesitation, and I was not prepared to subject myself to total annihilation.

It was the discovery of the cache of my personal letters, dating back to my time at university, that I found initially perplexing and then very disturbing. My father had highlighted different sections of these letters in three different colours, had noted if a page was missing and had frequently questioned the year in which the letter was written as many were only dated by day and month. The discovery of these highlighted letters made me feel very queasy. I frequently left personal letters and other papers in my bedroom at my parents' house when I stayed there during university holidays. Never did I think that my father would read them, let alone brazenly steal them. It was a shock to discover these letters in the file. Some of them were extremely personal and at times quite explicit. Did he get off sexually on reading them? I suspect so. A couple of letters alluded to sexual encounters with boyfriends and one in particular was very graphic. This sort of creepy voyeurism is a real violation and added yet another layer of abuse to that from which I had already been subjected.

The notes about telephone conversations with my siblings about me and my mental health were unexpected. The comments made by my siblings, as recorded by my father, were damning, describing me and my behaviour as 'basically selfish self-indulgence manipulative (underlined) histrionics' (4/5/79) and that I am 'intelligent but get something out of the manipulative histrionics' and 'drinking to excess'. The last at least was true. The notes are of conversations held during the late 1970s into the 1980s. This covers the period when I was drinking to excess and was in mental turmoil. If, as my sister once suggested in response to me expressing outrage at my father keeping these records, he kept notes because he was concerned about me, he certainly didn't express this concern or show any interest in my wellbeing at the time. I believe these records were kept solely for the purpose of discrediting me. I also believe it was in his best interest for me to keep abusing alcohol. Why else would he send me flowers when I was in hospital, after I had (permanently) stopped drinking, with a card that said, 'Even Bob Hawke fell off the wagon.'

My father only ever gave me advice on one occasion about how to succeed in the workforce. I cannot remember which job I was about to start or exactly what conversation we had been having, but I clearly remember him saying to me, 'Always be a good clerk.' By this I understood him to mean keep impeccable records. If I tease this counsel out a little further and combine it with his need to be in control, I think he also meant, 'And don't get caught out. Always have written evidence to back up your position.' It was very much in character for my father to gather information about me and keep it in order to discredit me and any allegations I might make about his incestuous behaviour. For him it was an insurance policy.

The timeline entitled 'Elizabeth – An Incomplete & Imprecise Chronology' was another interesting piece of factual information about me. It charts the years from my birth in 1944 until 1986, two years after I permanently gave up drinking alcohol in January 1984. The timeline records where I lived, the dates of my children's birth, my three marriages, along with some relationships, overdoses and hospitalisations and the DUI car crash. Apart from the births of my three children, it is a chronicle of disasters. It doesn't record achievements or successes. While they were few, they were hard won.

Perhaps that was the very point of the timeline.

The three newspaper cuttings on False Memory Syndrome Foundation (FMSF), initialled and dated by my father, appealed to my inner detective. The premise of the FMSF was that memories of abuse had been implanted in the victim's mind by an over-zealous and inadequately trained therapist. I googled FMSF to brush up on the Foundation and discovered that it had been dissolved in December 2019. I spent time reading the tweets of Dr Michael Salter, associate professor of Criminology, University of New South Wales. Salter is a researcher in a wide range of areas, all relating to violence against women, who refutes the position held by the FMSF. He is an advisor to the government on matters of violence against women and appeared on the ABC program Q&A to contribute to the current movement to bring about change regarding attitudes towards women. He strongly supports the achievement of social and economic equality across the board.

Salter states in a tweet on 30 December 2019 that 'The False Memory Syndrome Foundation is officially dissolved tomorrow. It was launched 27 years ago, claiming that adults disclosing child sexual abuse were suffering from a "syndrome" of vivid false memories of abuse.' Later in this same tweet, Salter states,

> *Much of the intellectual heft of the "false memory syndrome" movement came from the FMSF-aligned academics and lawyers who were paid to defend men accused of CSA (child sexual abuse) in court. The FMFS played a central role in matching accused abusers with defence lawyers and expert witnesses. This conflict of interest went largely unchallenged by journalists at the time.*

Finally, Salter states 'no such syndrome exists – it is, ironically enough, a false syndrome.'

I wasn't surprised that my father appeared to be drawn to the idea of 'false memories'. What better way to deny the incest, than by suggesting that the memories had been implanted by a counsellor or a therapist? As I read through the article he had underlined at different points, I could appreciate how persuasive an article it was. But it did not reference any reputable research and was largely anecdotal in the cases it reported. There is now an ever-increasing body of research into memory, traumatic memory, delayed memory and false memory.

I am not here to argue the case for or against the different types of memory, especially as I have experienced them all. I always remembered a molestation by the chemist boy when I was a small child in Canberra in 1948. I always knew my father had sexually abused me as a child, but my memory of the abuse took on different forms from always remembering, to auditory, visual and emotional flashback to a complete reliving. I had a crystal clear memory of the Rev Jack Tyrrell's predatory sexual behaviour when I was a vulnerable, young adult. And I have a memory of being with my mother in Tasmania when in fact I was alone with my father in Geneva. This creation of a false memory, which lasted for over four decades tells me the mind is capable of the most extraordinary things, much of it for protection of the individual.

One of the notes included in the file is of a drunken conversation I had with him on the phone in the early 1980s. When I read this note, part of me feels embarrassed, humiliated and ashamed. The other more compassionate part of me feels very sad for the survivor who was crying out to be heard and was trying to say something that was of enormous significance to her. How easy it is to dismiss things said when a person is drunk. I have always believed in the meaning of 'in vino veritas' (in wine there is truth). It just requires more effort to untangle what is really being said by the inebriated person.

The contents of the file still stir in me emotions that range from extreme anger to deep distress, against a background of confusion. The attitude conveyed by the contents is one of total disrespect for me as a person while dismissing my very essence as being of no importance. But for a fleeting moment, my cool analysis is still shaken when the long-ago child in me is overtaken by sadness that these documents reflect my father's view of me, his daughter.

How ironic that my father, the man for whom control and meticulous record-keeping were so important, should reveal himself in this way. His predatory behaviour and preoccupation with my sex life were there to be found in his own filing cabinet. Once I had processed everything the file told me, I knew I was looking at corroborating evidence.

> 1944 to 1956
>
> <u>Elizabeth</u>
> An Incomplete & Imprecise Chronology.
>
> 1944    Born
> 1953    To Geneva
> 1961    To Womens College.
> 1964    Married Sunday 7.
> 1965    Graduated BA/[...]
>          To New Zealand.
>          To USA Purdue
>          Kate & Andrew to NZ.
>          Divorced
> 1972    "Suicide attempt"
> 1973    Hip, on return from
>          Oxford, & Reg Committed
>          Liz to R.C.H : Out 19[..]
>          48 hours [...]
> 1974    Married Tony
> 1975 (17/2)    Emma born.
> 1980 (Aug)    Liz to Cabrery.
> 1980 (mid)    Living out.
> 1981 (Feb.)    Car smash.
> 1982 (31/7)    Announcement of engagement to York
> 1983    [...]
> 1984.    Kept tested
> 1985 (8/6)    [...]

*File excerpt: FHW's timeline of me.*

# Parents the latest victims of widespread sex abuse

*SMH 26/11/93*

How reliable is the mind in recalling abuse? **DENIS DUTTON** suggests, in some cases, false memory may be creating a new class of victims.

THE very idea of child sexual abuse provokes deep passions. On the one side there stands a profound impulse to protect vulnerable children from hideous crimes. Such feelings represent the best part of human nature but they can bring out the worst part as well: panic reactions that amount to little more than witch-hunts, with blameless families broken up (as in Britain) and innocent parents and child-care workers languishing in prison (as in the United States). Even if acquitted, victims' lives are left in tatters (as with the women falsely accused in a recent Christchurch creche case).

The stark reality and horror of child abuse, as the social psychologist Carol Tavris has pointed out, are such that considerable throat-clearing is required to raise even the slightest scepticism about its diagnosis and treatment.

Yet a failure critically to examine the more extreme claims of what she calls the "sex abuse industry" has created a whole new class of victims.

Consider the case of a retired Royal Navy officer summoned not long ago by his 28-year-old daughter to her London flat. Sitting in the lotus position, "Joanna", (the name given her by the British newspaper, *The Independent*), read him a statement describing how he had tickled her clitoris and stuck pencils in her vagina when she was less than a year old. When she was eight years old he had supposedly raped her orally and anally.

Later, Joanna "remembered" being molested by her grandfather and taken to a meeting where a baby was killed and men forced anal intercourse on her. With supporting letters from her therapist, she was now demanding £70,000 compensation from her father. He has refused and she has severed links with him, except for messages of swearing rage she leaves on his answering machine. These still reduce him to tears.

Joanna is not a victim of sexual abuse but rather has succumbed to the most vicious therapeutic trend of recent years. She is suffering from False Memory Syndrome, having been wrongly convinced by her therapist that she is an incest victim.

A typical case such as Joanna's begins when a client seeks counselling for a problem such as headaches or depression. Her (or his) therapist, persuaded by books such as *The Courage to Heal* by Bass and Davis, or Beverly Engel's *Right to Innocence*, has adopted the doctrine that undetected childhood sexual abuse causes many psychological malaises. The memory of abuse, these authors argue, is often repressed and unknown to the patient.

Confronted with the "reason" for her problems, the patient initially recoils in disbelief but, to the therapist, such denial is further proof that the sexual abuse is real.

Using hypnosis, the therapist urges the patient to recall the abuse and, by a process of suggestion and leading questions, both become convinced something terrible happened in her childhood. This in turn explains what is wrong in her life now.

Often, the pseudo-memories created in these sessions are revolting in their ugly detail. But sometimes they are based on definitions of sexual abuse so elastic they encourage clients to feel that anything their parent did that they didn't like was abuse. Beverly Engel disliked the way her mother would give her a "wet" kiss or walk in on her in the bathroom: "It was not until recently that I came to terms with my mother's behaviour and saw it for what it really was — sexual abuse."

In this climate of victim-worship, every annoyance or slight the mind can create or remember is elevated into a lasting grievance against parents.

Repeated memories "clarify" the traumatic memories, which are nothing more than fantasies based on the therapist's doctrines and line of questioning. To the vulnerable patient, however, it is all vividly real, and the establishment of a False

> *The aliens aren't on hand to be sued but mum and dad make perfect targets.*

Memory Syndrome (FMS) is complete.

The patient may take great consolation in procedure, discovering the reason for her current symptoms and achieving the status of victim-survivor. Certain of her condition, she confronts her stunned and bewildered parents, perhaps suing or demanding they be jailed. Though her family ties have been damaged irreparably, she now enjoys the care and love of her therapist and fellow-survivors (The therapeutic process may take time, however: one woman who subsequently sued her father had finally "remembered" his molestation in her 32nd therapy session.)

For students of the paranormal, this has a familiar ring. A decade ago, many people came to believe aliens were kidnapping ordinary citizens from their beds at night. Awakened by a blinding light, abduction victims were levitated out of the window by peculiar little beings with grey skin and large, black, Modigliani eyes. Once in the aliens' flying saucer, horrible medical experiments were performed on them, and women abductees were impregnated with alien embryos.

Most abduction "survivors" only understood their experiences after they had received attention from "expert" therapists trained (by reading the right books) to recognise the symptoms of UFO abduction. In fact, the same structure of practice and belief underlies both the misguided forms of the incest-sexual abuse industries and the UFO abduction industry. Patients suffering psychological distress are treated by therapists ideologically predisposed to a single cause for most of life's difficulties.

There is a crucial difference, however, between narratives of UFO abduction and fantasised sexual abuse. The aliens aren't on hand to be sued but mum and dad, if they're still in the neighbourhood, make perfect targets.

Of course, sexual abuse is a demonstrably real crime in New Zealand [and Australia] today. But, in our anxiety about it we must not create a whole new class of victims: parents and family members falsely accused of sexual abuse by younger people suffering from FMS.

The key delusion on which FMS is founded is the notion that traumatic memories are often "repressed" and can be recovered decades later by hypnosis. There is no evidence whatsoever for general repression of major life-events, and certainly not for highly traumatic experiences. One study of children who had witnessed the murder of a parent showed that none had repressed the memory. Children who were in concentration camps cannot rid themselves of the memory. The question for true victims of sexual abuse is not, "how can I remember it?" but rather, "how can I forget it?"

Recent psychological studies have shown how easy it is to inject false memories into people's minds simply by asking questions ("remember when you were little and lost in the shopping mall?"). Far from improving memory, hypnosis tends to render subjects more suggestible while making pseudo-memories more vivid.

The old idea, popular in the 1960s, that hypnotism can improve recall, for example, enabling crime witnesses to remember briefly-glimpsed licence numbers, has by now been thoroughly tested and refuted but it is still treated as a valid doctrine by some sexual-abuse counsellors.

More than 4,000 distraught families have so far contacted the False Memory Syndrome Foundation in Philadelphia, formed, as the founder, Martin Gardner, explains, "to combat a fast-growing epidemic of dubious therapy that is ripping thousands of families apart, scarring patients for life, and breaking the hearts of innocent relatives". Mr Gardner calls FMS "the mental-health crisis of the 1990s".

FMS represents a threat to every loving, normal parent whose child might some day, encountering a rough patch, fall into the hands of a therapist who accepts the myths of memory repression and hypnotic enhancement. It is up to educated, enlightened psychologists and health professionals to see that this is one fad that does not become established in Australia and New Zealand. Sexual abuse — a real and terrible crime — creates enough victims as it is.

*These remarks, by philosopher Denis Dutton of New Zealand's University of Canterbury, are extracted from the annual President's Lecture at the Christchurch School of Medicine.*

*File excerpt: False Memory Syndrome newspaper clipping.*

*File note:*
*½ pissed; Downer; Washing floors etc – 7 days;*
*Sexually frigid – all Thru the 20 years Sandy – Tony – Gordon*
*Some sort of a block (Earlier reference 'I freeze up')*

> What else can I say, Elizabeth ? Life without men would become even more complicated ! Sorry the above paragraph was a bit crude but I presume that you have by now a good (academic at least ) knowledge of Sex And All That... And if and when that knowledge becomes a wee bit less academic, your enjoyment and comprehension of life and Life will increase immesurably but so will the problems. Going to bed with someone rarely if ever solves problems existing in other departments of a relationship but, if it is the right kind and going well, it has its undeniable worth. This said in case that eventuality comes over the horizon in the more or less immediate future..... and it is something that no

*Letter I received from Pierre, with FHW's underlines and highlighting*

'burnt' this letter) and then ejaculated, and I think the only reason he managed that much, was because we'd had so much sex together previously, and so, wouldn't have been quite as worked up as Sandy was. But it often happens hair-pre-ejac I mean. So the thing to do now is, as you said — make sure he feels it doesn't matter. Next time — have a nice quiet place, and lots and lots of time, and make him go very slowly, and kiss you a lot first, and take it all very gently and quietly — try not to let him get too passionate — I mean not passionate I mean. Also tell him before that you're not going to have an orgasm whatever he does probably, because

*Letter I received from my friend Anne, with my father's underlining*

# To the Edge and Back

In December 2009, only weeks before I was due to retire, I was diagnosed with breast cancer. I reacted with the predictable feelings of shock, disbelief and eventually acceptance and a 'let's get on with it' approach. I also did a mental stocktake of unfinished business in my life as I grew up in a time when cancer was regarded as a death sentence. Near the top of the list was my long-held ambition to write a memoir about the incest that had so affected my life. Soon after I completed my cancer treatment, I enthusiastically joined a writers' group started by a friend and former colleague. Called Scribblers, the group was an ideal setting to start writing my story. It was small, safe, and supportive. The words flowed relatively easily and my fellow writers listened attentively to each instalment I read out.

As I grew stronger with the passing months, the urgency of my mission diminished and I spent less time writing. It felt like my cancer episode was behind me and life returned to normal. That all changed when four years later, I was diagnosed with an aggressive form of leukaemia.

In July 2014, my younger daughter Emma and I had a wonderful holiday in Bali. It was a destination we had been to several times before and we had grown to love the people and the richness of the culture. After the holiday was over, we took the overnight flight from Denpasar to Darwin before continuing our drive south to Katherine. I was to stay with

Emma for a few days before returning to Canberra. I remember distinctly when we reached Adelaide River, roughly the half-way mark, and we stopped to buy some drinks. I was at the point of vomiting I was so exhausted. I had never experienced feeling so completely drained that I had nothing left in reserve. I caught up on some rest in Katherine but decided to keep an eye on my extreme feelings of tiredness.

I found it impossible to judge just how serious my level of fatigue was, so I battled through the next couple of months until it became obvious that I needed to get checked out medically. I made an appointment with my doctor Suzanne, who ordered blood tests. I will always remember that it was a Friday in October when Suzanne rang to say the test results had shown abnormalities in the white cells and she wanted the tests to be repeated straight after the weekend. I spent Saturday and Sunday googling the possible causes for abnormal white cells. Leukaemia came up as a strong candidate. The Monday blood test confirmed my worst fear. I was told to go to Accident and Emergency and admit myself to hospital the next day. With acute myeloid leukaemia (AML) the blast (cancer) cells multiply rapidly and it is crucial to begin treatment as soon as possible after diagnosis. Even though I didn't fully understand how this disease operated, I was caught up in the gravity of what was unfolding as I packed a few essentials for hospital. Following this, events moved rapidly.

Once I had been admitted I gladly entered the hospital bubble where everyday reality ceased to exist, and hospital routine and medical procedures took over. It was like moving into a dreamlike state where nothing was quite real.

Soon after my admission I had a meeting with all the haematology staff involved in my care. Emma was with me as both support person and another pair of ears. My memory of this meeting is that it all seemed very positive until the end when the odds of survival, as they were spelt out, were not good. Emma and I sat there, looking at one another in disbelief and we both burst into tears. Treatment, being three rounds of harsh chemotherapy, was to be started after a central line was inserted, into which the chemo would be administered. Through the haze that softened all that was happening, I remember thinking to myself, 'surely it can't be much worse than the final round of chemo for the breast cancer.' That had pushed me right to the limit. I had told my oncologist I didn't think I could do it. He resolved my dilemma by decreasing the strength of the chemo. And I did get through it! I superimposed that memory onto the AML treatment, rather too optimistically as it turned out.

I was really scared about having the central line inserted. I remember being wheeled by a cheerful wardsman down the long, hospital corridors to the room where this procedure was to take place. I showed my vulnerability as I asked the anaesthetist, a woman, if I could hold someone's hand during the procedure, as I was terrified. She looked at me with understanding and told me that because it was imperative that the sterile conditions be maintained, she couldn't oblige, but she would communicate with her eyes. I was given some form of sedative which smoothed the edges of my terror, but as I looked at my surroundings all I could see were masks and shrouds covering everyone and everything. Apart from the doctors and nurses' eyes being visible and machines displaying their data in bright colours, everything was covered in pure, white cloth.

It was as if all humanity had been sucked out of the room. I felt terribly alone. Then, unexpectedly, I felt a hand squeeze my calf and let it go. Then another squeeze and I began to let go of all the fear and tension. With each squeeze I let go just a little more, and in my woozy brain thought, how wonderful that someone had bent the rules and reached out to make contact. I focused on this human reassurance to get through the procedure. It was not until much later that I learnt my source of comfort had been, in fact, a mechanical cuff monitoring my blood pressure.

During my time in hospital, I was moved around the cancer ward and into several different rooms, including a spell in isolation when the chemo had reduced my immunity to a very low level. It is only by reading my discharge summary that I am reminded of different segments of the month-long hospitalisation. There is a blurriness surrounding this episode of my life and I became quite robotic in my responses except when I had to decide whether to continue the prescribed three rounds of chemotherapy after the first round almost killed me. Even this critical moment is a bit hazy around the edges.

During my first round of chemo I found myself in a windowless room with curtained cubicles which housed approximately eight cancer patients. My little cubicle was just near the entrance to the ward which was fortunate as the chemo was accompanied by violent diarrhoea which had resulted in all sorts of mishaps as I tried to manage the various intravenous lines attached to a selection of upside-down bottles of life-supporting fluids.

I was confined to my hospital bed with its crisp white sheets and the mandatory blue coverlet. The bed consumed most of the space, leaving just enough room on my right for the bedside cabinet and the brown laminate table-on-wheels required for meal trays and the endless bottles of water I was cajoled into drinking. On my left there was a single chair and a skinny white cupboard for the clothes I had worn when I was admitted to hospital. This area was my personal space even though it was only separated from the other patients by a flimsy blue curtain that pretended to afford privacy but in reality, didn't. Sounds and conversations passed through and offered both intrusion and, at times, companionship. Across from my cubicle was a middle-aged woman who was very vocal and optimistic despite the poor prognosis she told me about. She was a larger-than-life figure who, during a quiet time late at night, announced very loudly that she had to get rid of the terrible build-up of wind in her abdomen, and though very apologetic, would just have to... 'LET IT RIP!'

While I was in this ward my brother Philip, who lives in Sydney but was visiting his daughter and her family just outside Canberra, offered to come into the hospital and sit with me for the time he was visiting. He made it clear he would make no demands on me and would sit quietly with his laptop attending to various tasks. I flashed back to my father visiting me daily, at lunchtime, in the Calvary hospital psychiatric ward, and how silent and threatening that had been. So, even as I accepted this generous offer, I was filled with trepidation. But it was an entirely different experience and I remember it with great warmth. I found my brother's presence, day after day, gently supportive as he sat in the somewhat cramped space, working away on his laptop. He gave me, most unexpectedly, true caring and reassurance. He was there to bounce off the decisions I had to make, and yet he never tried to influence me one way or another.

There must have been some humour even in those dire circumstances, for our past relationship had always been based in part, on seeing the funny side of any situation. Such was the atmosphere of trust that I confessed to a lie I had told him some sixty years before and about which I had always felt extremely guilty. I had been very jealous of the obvious affection our mother showed him. So, one morning, as we walked to school from our apartment in Avenue William Favre, I told him how I knew Mum really didn't love him that much. This reduced him to tears. It was a cruel and nasty thing to do and didn't make me feel any more loved by our mother. So, in the spirit of trust and the hovering shadow of my death, I told him how I had lied to him all those years before. The sweet irony was that he had no memory whatsoever of the incident. These two weeks remain with me as confirmation of a sibling bond that is strong and enduring.

As with my diagnosis and treatment for breast cancer, my children were with me every inch of the way. Emma came with clean nighties for me, day after day. Patients, in their need to have contact with the outside world, forget that it is very tiring for family members who are working day jobs, to visit after work. I always wanted Emma to stay a little longer. It was another time my feeling of aloneness surged to the fore.

I was faced with deciding whether or not to continue with the treatment. My copy of the medical report that my doctor Suzanne Davey sent to Care Oncology in the UK tells me that my close encounter with death had been due to severe sepsis and a lung abscess. I was in yet another ward, early in my treatment, when I was admitted to ICU following a 'medical emergency'. I do remember the room filling with the entire medical team explaining to me what was happening. And yet what I recall most vividly is a voice in my head that said, 'you can go left, or you can go right.' I chose to go right... and I lived.

After this episode, I knew at a gut level I would not survive another round of chemotherapy. The near-death experience I had been through underscored my own mortality. I also resolved to complete my story.

A crucial turning point in my treatment happened when Andrew phoned a friend of his, Greg Stoloff, in the United Kingdom. Greg was a former investment banker who had changed career direction and was now deeply involved in cancer research. He believed his talent for solving complex financial conundrums, could be used to tackle some of the more difficult healthcare issues. Andrew contacted Greg and explained my predicament. He asked if the treatment he was trialling through his healthcare startup, Care Oncology, would be worth considering. The treatment was an adjunctive therapy which involved using repurposed medicines to target the cancer at a metabolic level. His response was decisive. He recommended that I start the treatment immediately. The protocol he was suggesting was unproven, but Greg was very confident that it was worth trying, especially given my decision to discontinue the chemo.

Andrew coordinated communication between Greg and my GP Suzanne, and I started on the protocol within a couple of days. I didn't realise just how precarious my situation was, nor that my treating haematologist had washed his hands of me when I wouldn't agree to his chemo-focused treatment plan. It seemed to me that the haematologist cared more about adhering to his rigid approach than he did about whether his patients lived or died. This still causes me enormous anger.

I was discharged without being fully aware of my poor prognosis. Suzanne, my doctor of many years, agreed to supervise me on the Care Oncology protocol and prescribe the medication. During this time I had a long phone consultation with one of the Care Oncology Team and I found this contact enormously informative and encouraging.

It is now over a decade since my acute myeloid leukaemia diagnosis. I understand my haematologist gave me approximately six weeks to live after I declined to continue with the chemo.

As a result of my AML experience, I become very scared if I encounter a period of excessive tiredness for no apparent reason. I start to believe that I am relapsing, which inevitably leads to thoughts of death. When I have reached a place of 'needing' an answer, I make an appointment with my doctor to ask for the blood test which will reveal any abnormal white cells. This seems to happen about once a year and is part and parcel of being a cancer survivor. When I contemplate my death, I think about what it would mean for those close to me, as well as for myself. And this leads me to reflect on those people and activities I most value in my life, as well as reflecting on what I have experienced and overcome and what I have achieved.

*Sharing a joke with Andrew in the courtyard of the Canberra Hospital as I began my leukaemia treatment*

# In My Garden

When I was in my thirties and early forties, I would scour the local bookshops for memoirs written by abuse survivors. I did so as unobtrusively as possible. I felt very exposed because of the heavy mantle of shame I carried from my own experiences. I was sure people next to me in the aisles would notice which books I was looking for and would think me disgusting or perverted for wanting to read accounts of child sexual abuse. These were the early years of me acknowledging the wide-ranging impact the incest had on every aspect of my life. When I unexpectedly came across a memoir written by a survivor, I felt excited anticipation as I paid for it. I hoped that it would speak to me and validate me in a way I had not yet dared ask for in real life. I tentatively raised the topic with a few of the psychiatrists I saw, but other than Dr Maxine Tenant, I don't remember any mental health professional responding in a meaningful way. My disclosure was dismissed as unimportant so I looked to books for the reassurance I needed. Reading the stories of other abuse survivors encouraged me. I was not alone. I was not crazy.

As I moved beyond that vulnerable and lonely place, I began to think about writing my own story. Survivors have such a lot to tell each other and through sharing our stories, we can affirm the experiences with each other, as well as offering new insights and understanding. This isn't surprising given that trauma does manifest in a similar way even when the sources of the trauma may be different.

In recent years I have become acutely aware of just how much my father's abuse impacted relationships and, indirectly, my ability to parent. As was clear from my first marriage at the age of twenty, the damage was unmistakable. I was shocked and saddened as I realised the extent of the fallout and accompanying losses. I took charge in small increments over long periods of time and made progress. I made an enormous effort and commitment to overcome the mental health problems that restricted my freedom of movement. I became sober. I attended the group for overcoming agoraphobia, after which I was successful in gaining meaningful employment as a social worker. I completed the Fearless Flyers course, so I could be at Kate's wedding in Auckland. This was followed by even more bold and exciting international travel with Emma and Andrew.

Therapeutic groups allowed me to break free from the mental cage that held me captive for so long and were the outward signs of recovery. I could reach out to the world, once more. The feeling was extraordinary. The real, day-to-day work continued in a much quieter way and involved getting through the horrendous lows, changing medication which usually entailed unpleasant withdrawal and persisting through flashbacks and nightmares... not giving up during times that challenged every fibre of my being.

I am proud of what I've achieved. I was very difficult to live with at times and I remember the dark periods of depression feeling like they would never end. They filled me with guilt, as an all-pervading message in my family of origin was that only a positive outlook was acceptable. *No black clouds.*

I had an unrelenting need to confront my father about the incest. I needed a response in writing. I harboured this very small hope that my father would acknowledge the incest and apologise. He did not. He denied my allegations through his solicitor with carefully chosen words. Much earlier I had believed I needed to remember the sexual acts he perpetrated in minute detail in order to be freed from the damage. I was wrong about that. I also had to relinquish the belief that an acknowledgement, combined with an apology, was required for me to be normal. Many survivors of incest share this misguided view.

When my father died, I received substantial validation from the contents of the file he kept about me. This gave me a disturbing look into his voyeuristic fixation on my relationships with men and my sex life. It took me a very long time to process this information but eventually it helped me to find the beginning of the peace I sought.

I had three aims uppermost in my mind when I embarked on my memoir. I wanted to help my children understand why I was not able to look after them when they were little and I wanted them to know that my failings were never deliberate. It was also very important that I share my story with other survivors. Perhaps I could offer some support and hope and encouragement in the same way I had been given so much help through earlier memoirs I had read. I also wanted to draw attention to incest.

The mention of incest elicits a different type of response than other child sexual abuse offences. It comes with a disturbing disquiet that most people don't want to face. People's responses can also be explained in terms of the closeness of family relationships. Sexual abuse of a child by a father or older brother or uncle or other family member is particularly difficult to understand. Society tells us in so many ways, and through advertising in particular, that families nurture, look after and protect children. They don't wilfully harm them. Incest, most notably, defies society's norms, thereby creating a threat. People go into denial and pretend it doesn't exist. But it absolutely does. The real incidence of incest is likely to be much higher than reported for many reasons. Often family exerts pressure to 'not tell', or the victim responds to threats by the perpetrator, or is conflicted by feelings of loyalty to a parent, uncle or grandfather. The idea of family, however dysfunctional, is very powerful.

My experience of very early molestation by the chemist boy and the adult experience of grooming and molestation by the Rev Jack Tyrrell left me with a feeling of disgust and being used. It did not, however, damage my very being, as my father's abuse did. This has led me to believe that it is imperative to bring incest into the conversation, as a first step.

We need to remove the wall of silence that protects perpetrators. Incest belongs in the field of family violence, which is very slowly gaining more attention and people are taking it more seriously.

I know how difficult it will be for some incest survivors to bring the spotlight onto their suffering. It has taken me a lifetime to gain the confidence and find the courage to name the abuse and to talk openly about my father.

I'm often reminded of TS Eliot's quote from Little Gidding.

*We shall not cease from exploration. And the end of all our exploring. Will be to arrive where we started. And know the place for the first time.*

Another important part of my healing process has been the coming together of my children. It has happened over many years by naming the separation and the events surrounding it and sharing some of the pain. I salute the capacity of the truth to make way for love, clarity and real connection.

For me, finding peace is not dramatic, but gradual. In recent years I've noticed the sunsets seem to be more powerful. I see them in a way I never have before. I watch them from my back steps as they slide into darkness.

Peace is having a clear head instead of worries careering around your brain searching for a solution. It is heading out to my garden to be with the plants I have nurtured and to let whatever was overwhelming me gently float away. It is quiet moments of reflection. It is just being. My life is much calmer with less extremes of mood. It's not perfect, and I wouldn't want it to be, but it no longer hurts as it used to.

*Turning 70 and celebrating with my children in Fiji*

*With Kate and Emma in Fiji*

# Epilogue

On a Saturday morning in September 2020, I returned a call to my sister expecting no more than to pass the time of day and perhaps exchange news of our children. Instead, the conversation veered off in an unanticipated direction when I spoke of my Covid-related projects, gardening and writing my memoir. My sister asked what my memoir was about, to which I replied, that it was about the sexual abuse perpetrated on me by my father.

Throughout my life I have been unable to discuss the details of the abuse – or the effects – with my brother and sister. It was a dark unspoken truth I had to deal with on my own.

We spoke on the phone for over two hours, in which time my sister asked me more direct and detailed questions about my abuse than she had ever asked before and showed genuine interest in my replies. Our conversation culminated with her suggestion that we arrange a get-together with our brother, so that we could share our individual stories of growing up in our family of origin.

I agreed, and prior to our meeting, I emailed a copy of my draft memoir and requested that they both read it before we met.

It was not the meeting itself that brought about extraordinary change, although it did reveal an openness that wasn't there previously. The change was expressed in an email I received on 11 January from my brother. He had read my memoir more than once; he listened, and he heard. Philip was very clear that his experience of childhood was very different to mine. His was a happy one. But in that moment when we were together, I sensed that he believed me. I believe that he absorbed my story at a deep level. He referred to it often during the meeting while the three of us talked about various aspects of our upbringing.

For the first time in my life, the truth was acknowledged by my own family.

My father, once referred to in venerated terms, was now referred to in a markedly different way. I didn't participate a great deal. I didn't need to. I had already had my say.

# Timeline

- Father Fred born: 9 January 1914
- Mother Peggy born: 28 September 1914
- Sister Pam born: 4 March 1941
- I was born: 9 January 1944
- Brother Philip born: 1 December 1947
- Left Canberra for Geneva: end 1952
- Final year of school: 1959/60
- Left Geneva, return to Australia: end of 1960
- Started at Sydney University, living in Women's College: March 1961
- First marriage: 22 August 1964
- Moved to Rotorua, New Zealand May 1965
- Daughter Kate born: 1 October 1965
- Son Andrew born: 21 February 1968
- Left Rotorua, moved to Lafayette, Indiana USA: August 1969
- Returned to Canberra from Lafayette: June 1970 – stayed with parents
- Moved into flat in Red Hill, Canberra, late 1970
- Reconciliation trip in Fiji: summer 1970–71
- Lived in Young NSW: summer 1971–72
- Lived in Bowral NSW: 1972
- Moved back to Canberra: 1972
- Bought house in Curtin and move in with Kate and Andrew: 1972
- Sister-in-law stayed with me for brief period: 1972
- Stress breakdown; Kate and Andrew to Mittagong with father 1972
- Overdose resulting in hospital admission: 1972

- Election party: December 1972
- Moved in with friends, Anne and Philip: 1973
- Started work as Employment Officer CCAE: 1973
- Kate and Andrew to New Zealand with their father: 1973
- Overdose resulting in hospital admission: 1973
- Met Tony and become pregnant with Emma: early–mid 1974
- Second marriage to Tony: November 1974
- Daughter Emma born: 17 February 1975
- Death of mother Peggy: 18 November 1975
- Started work with TAFE Reid employed as psychologist: 1976
- Overdose resulting in hospital admission: 1978
- Started work as social worker Paediatrics WVH: 1980
- Overdose resulting in hospital admission: 1980
- Started work as Welfare Officer Canberra Birthright: 1982
- Overdose resulting in hospital admission: 1982
- Started work as Welfare Officer Woden Senior Citizens Club: 1985
- Third marriage: 23 January 1987
- Started work as social worker Narrabundah Health Centre: 1989
- Started work as social worker Phillip Health Centre: 1992
- Legal Aid letter from Chris Staniforth, on my behalf, to my father regarding allegations of sexual abuse by me: 13/7/1993
- Reply from my father to Legal Aid denying any truth in allegations: 6/8/1993
- Death of father: 5 August 1994
- Funeral: Discovery of file my father kept about me – 8 August 1994
- Started work as social worker Tuggeranong Health Centre: 2011

# Helplines in Australia

Helplines for survivors who are in crisis, or needing to talk:

**Lifeline**
    Phone: 13 11 14 24/7 Crisis Support
    Text Support: Text a Lifeline counsellor 24/7 at 0477 13 11 14

**National Domestic Family and Sexual Violence Counselling Service**
    Phone: 1800 RESPECT (1800 737 732) (24 hours)
    Text Support: 0458 737 732 (24 hours)

**Healthdirect Australia Sexual assault and rape - helplines, definition, reporting**
    Phone: 1800 022 222 (24 hours) – *ask for assistance with referral to a health service. This includes services for sexual assault and rape.*
    Website: https://www.healthdirect.gov.au

**Blue Knot Foundation**
    Phone: 1300 657 380 Monday to Sunday 9am – 5pm
    Email: helpline@blueknot.org.au

# References

**Recommended books**
Susan Forward, *Toxic Parents: Overcoming their hurtful legacy and reclaiming your life*, Bantam Dell, 2002
Judith Herman, *Trauma and Recovery: The aftermath of violence—from domestic abuse to political terror*, Sage, 2015
Judith Herman, *Father–Daughter Incest*, Harvard University Press, 2000
Aphrodite Matsakis, *I Can't Get Over It: A handbook for trauma survivors*, New Harbinger, 1996
Bessel van der Kolk, *The Body Keeps the Score: Brain, mind, and body in the healing of trauma*, Penguin, 2015

**Non-fiction and Memoir**
Gemma Carey, *No Matter our Wreckage: A memoir about grooming, betrayal, trauma and love.* Allen & Unwin, 2020
Jane Caro, ed., *Unbreakable: Women share stories of resilience and hope*, University of Queensland Press, 2017
Sylvia Fraser, *In My Father's House: A memoir of incest and healing*, Virago, 1996
Clark Fredericks, *Scarred*, Simon Schuster, 2025
Amy Griffin, *The Tell*, Penguin, 2025
Judy King, *Agnes – A childhood betrayed and reclaimed*, Ginninderra Press, 2024
Cathy Ann Mathews, *Breaking Through: No longer a victim of child abuse*, Strand Publishing, 2011
James M Miller, *The Priests*, Finch, 2016
Lucia Osborne-Crowley, *I Choose Elena: On Trauma, Memory, and Survival*, The Indigo Press, 2020
Jane Rowan, *The River of Forgetting: A memoir of healing from sexual abuse*, Ginger Cat/Booksmyth Press, 2010
Jessica Stern, *Denial: A memoir of terror*, HarperCollins, 2010
Grace Tame, *The Ninth Life of a Diamond Miner: A memoir*, Macmillan, 2022

**Books that give an insight into the legal system and how survivors are being treated**

Hayley Boxall, Adam Tomison and Shann Hulme, *Historical review of sexual offence and child sexual abuse legislation in Australia: 1788–2013*, Australian Institute of Criminology, 2014

Bri Lee, *Eggshell Skull*, Allen & Unwin, 2018

Louise Milligan, *Witness,* Hachette, 2020

**Other references cited**

Australian Broadcasting Corporation, *Conversations with Richard Fidler and Sarah Kanowski*, 'Sisonke Msimang: Freedom's child', ABC Radio, https://www.youtube.com/watch?v=GHFlK2g9j80

Australian Bureau of Statistics, *Characteristics and outcomes of childhood abuse,* Australian Bureau of Statistics (https://www.abs.gov.au), released 6 May 2019

Australian Government Publishing Service, *1976 Royal Commission into Human Relationships,* https://apo.org.au/node/34438

John Cantwell, *Exit Wounds: One Australian's war on terror,* Melbourne University Publishing, 2013

Claudia Herrera Hudson, *My Hero* website, https://myhero.com/Dolores_Olmedo_Patino (description of Dolores Olmedo)

Derek Llewellyn-Jones, *Everywoman*, Penguin, 1998 (1971)

AM Jones, *Exposure Therapy and Coping Tactics,* p.3

Gabor Maté, *The Wisdom of Trauma*, https://thewisdomoftrauma.com/

JR Nethercote, 'Unearthing the Seven Dwarfs and the Age of the Mandarins', *Australian Dictionary of Biography,* National Centre of Biography, 2012

*Hidden Epidemic*, p. 163 and The Journal of Adolescent Health, January 2017 (puberty in girls sexually abused in childhood)

Michael Salter, *The privatisation of incest: the neglect of familial sexual abuse in Australian public inquiries*, Western Sydney University Research Direct

Michael Salter, @mike_salter, 30 December 2019 https://twitter.com/mike_salter/status/1211442594821001216?lang=en (dissolution of False Memory Syndrome Foundation)

Benjamin Spock, *Baby and Child Care*, Gallery Books, 2018 (1946)

Oprah Winfrey, *People*, 4 March 2018 (abuse and complicity)

# References cited by chapter

**Epigraph**
Special thanks to the Baldwin Estate for permission to use the opening quote from the essay *As Much Truth as One Can Bear.*
James Baldwin, *As Much Truth as One Can Bear,* The New York Times Book Review, January 14, 1962.

**Introduction**
Australian Institute of Criminology Special Report, *Historical review of sexual offence and child sexual abuse legislation in Australia: 1788–2013.* (records dating from colonisation).
Peter Freyd founded the False Memory Syndrome Foundation (FMSF) in 1992. The claims made by the FMSF for the incidence and prevalence of false memories have been criticised as lacking evidence and disseminating alleged inaccurate statistics about the problem. FMSF was dissolved in 2019.
Judith Herman, *Trauma and Recovery*, Chapter 5, p. 98. (fear maintaining silence in child sexual abuse)
Bessel van der Kolk, *The Body Keeps the Score,* Chapter 11. (memory fragments as part of the trauma narrative)
Grace Tame, *Press Club Address,* March 2021. (Grace Tame, a voice for survivors)

**The Move to Geneva**
Bessel van der Kolk, *The Body Keeps the Score*, Chapter 10, *Developmental Trauma: The Hidden Epidemic*, p. 163 and *The Journal of Adolescent Health*, January 2017 (puberty in girls sexually abused in childhood)
Claudia Herrera Hudson, *My Hero* website, https://myhero.com/Dolores_Olmedo_Patino (description of Dolores Olmedo)

**The Approaching Storm**
John Cantwell, *Exit Wounds*, pp. 351–2 (PTSD and effect on driving)

**The Gynaecologist**
Judith Herman, *Father–Daughter Incest* (secrecy imposed by the perpetrator)

**Searching for Answers**
Gabor Maté, *The Wisdom of Trauma*, https://thewisdomoftrauma.com/ (manifestation of trauma as mental illness and addiction)

**The Twilight Zone**
Bessel van der Kolk, *The Body Keeps the Score*, Part 4, *The Imprint of Trauma* (flashbacks)
Susan Forward, *Toxic Parents,* Chapter 7, *The Ultimate Betrayal,* (dysfunctional families)
**Memories Told in Flashback**
Bessel van der Kolk, *The Body Keeps the Score,* Part 4, *The Imprint of Trauma* (storing memories)
**Crawling to the Letterbox**
AM Jones, *Exposure Therapy and Coping Tactics,* p.3
**Shame**
ABC Radio National, *Conversations with Richard Fidler and Sarah Kanowski,* 'Sisonke Msimang: Freedom's child', 27 July 2022 (shame, acknowledgement and apology)
Oprah Winfrey, *People*, 4 March 2018 (abuse and complicity)
**Not Being Believed**
*Characteristics and outcomes of childhood abuse*, Australian Bureau of Statistics (https://www.abs.gov.au)
1976 Royal Commission into Human Relationships, https://apo.org.au/node/34438
Salter, M. (2016) *The privatisation of incest: The neglect of familial sexual abuse in Australian public inquiries,* Chapter 8, Findlay, M, Kaladelfos, A, & Smaal, Y, T*he sexual abuse of children: Recognition and redress*. Monash University Press: Melbourne
**Reflections on My Mother**
Benjamin Spock, *Baby and Child Care*
**Reflections on My Father**
Judith Herman, *Father–Daughter Incest*, Chapter 5, 'The Perpetrator: His Characteristics and Modus Operandi'
**The Funeral and the Wake**
JR Nethercote, 'Unearthing the Seven Dwarfs and the Age of the Mandarins', *Australian Dictionary of Biography*, 5 October 2012
Michael Salter, @mike_salter, 30 December 2019, (dissolution of False Memory Syndrome Foundation)
**In My Garden**
TS Eliot's *Little Gidding* http://www.columbia.edu/itc/history/winter/w3206/edit/tseliotlittlegidding.html

## Acknowledgements

I could never have imagined how much support and encouragement I would receive from my children and my friends for telling my story of incest and child sexual abuse. It has been heartwarming for me and a ray of hope for changes in attitude and understanding in the wider community.

**Angela Nordlinger** – thank you for believing me and believing in me. You put so much time and energy into editing that first draft and you were always supportive thereafter.

**Marie Jamieson** – my deepest thanks for a friendship that started at Narrabundah Health Centre and continued into our lives beyond that time. You always listened carefully, and you supported me through some really tough times. And here we are, both still standing!

My deep and sincere thanks to **Anne le Couteur** and **Barb Day** for reading two drafts of my memoir and giving me enough feedback and encouragement to keep on going early on when I was still full of doubts Reading two drafts was a big ask and your feedback was invaluable.

Scribblers – **Anne and Jenny**. You listened to my first rough attempts to tell my story and encouraged me to continue. I appreciate that so much.

My deepest thanks to my doctor of 20 plus years, **Suzanne Davey,** for believing me and supporting me through some really difficult times and cheering me on when I succeeded. I was so fortunate to find you.

To **Helen Garner**, your encouragement meant the world to me.

To my friends from Women's College with whom I share a wonderful friendship that has grown since our early hopeful days in college when we thought all things were possible.

To the new – now old – friends from my time in Health who never questioned the truth of the incest and were always supportive and non-judgemental when I struggled.

Finally, to my three adult children Kate, Andrew and Emma and my granddaughter Claudia for being there. Your presence in my life gives me strength and meaning.

www.ingramcontent.com/pod-product-compliance
Lightning Source LLC
Chambersburg PA
CBHW060353080526
44583CB00012B/288